PAULINE FURNESS

ROLE PLAY IN THE ELEMENTARY SCHOOL

A HANDBOOK FOR TEACHERS

112212

HART PUBLISHING COMPANY, INC.
NEW YORK CITY

Contents

Introduction

I am excited that this book is now available for both teachers to use in their classrooms, as well as school counselors to use with special groups of children. It spells out procedures that all teachers can readily put into practice that not only make academic learning more fun, but also provide for the introduction of human relations skills learning in a manner that seems far more constructive and relevant to the changing times than the procedures widely used in the schools today.

I first learned about Pauline Furness's unique contribution to classroom learning when she was finishing her undergraduate degree at CSUN, several years ago. At that time she was doing a demonstration program using her role-playing techniques with a group of difficult children in an elementary school where I was supervising our school psychologist trainees in their field placement. I was impressed with the changes that I saw in these children as a result of her utilization of simplified theatrical procedures in a group setting. One child who could readily be labelled recessive was actively participating in the group by "playing" the role of someone not herself. Other children who were known for their aggressive behavior were becoming aware of what it was like to be on the receiving end of their own behavior as they learned other ways of solving personal dilemmas via the role-playing procedures and the discussions which followed each of the sessions.

Since that time, Ms. Furness has completed her doctorate in Human Behavior, has conducted many classes with teachers on the use of Role-Playing procedures and has experimented with other dramatic means for enhancing learning with children. Prior to entering her doctoral program, Dr. Furness taught a sixth grade class for one year during which time she utilized the procedures she has written up here as a part of the daily activities of her classroom. Thus she knows from firsthand experience what it is like to use role-playing with a regular classroom of forty students. While there, other teachers became intrigued with what was going on in her class and asked her to spell out what she did. School psychologist trainees were also given an opportunity to explore the role-playing skits in group counseling situations. Thus the procedures have been tried out by a large number of teachers and other professionals in the schools. The enthusiasm on the part of these people has provided the background for the publication of this book. The themes are suitable for students from kindergarten through the twelfth grade, and cover the gamut of human relations issues found among them, as well as procedures for making it more interesting and possibly more efficient to learn academic skills such as arithmetic and spelling.

Pauline Furness entered the fields of education and psychology from a theatrical background. As a child actress she had the opportunity to learn about the personal growth potential in acting the role of the other. In the course of her growing up she became aware of the range of human dilemmas people encounter and the myriad of ways in which people attempt to resolve them. When Dr. Furness became interested in the field of education, it was to her great credit that she incorporated her theatrical talents and know-how into the daily procedures of the classroom. For she was aware of how much children enjoy dramatics, and how useful this love of dramatics can be for learning skills in interpersonal relations - something that is not regarded as terribly important by most school personnel. By introducing the problems that children run into with one another and with adults, not only in school but also on the outside, she has provided a way for humanizing classroom life.

One of the saddening aspects of many classrooms even today is that they are an encapsulated environment where people, both teachers and students, are expected to act as if they are not human. Thus there are many children who do not know that teachers are human beings like themselves who engage in the same kind of activities necessary for survival on the outside that the children do themselves. Teachers are not only discouraged from disclosing these basic aspects of their own humanness but are often discouraged from being openly emotionally expressive. It almost seems as if the more they act like robots the better they are as teachers! The introduction of role-playing procedures into the ongoing activities of the regular class puts the stamp of approval on being expressive as well as on learning what kinds of expressiveness produce desirable consequences. In addition, it provides an opportunity to know what it feels like to be in the role of the other. Thus, it provides a basis for empathy training and the beginning of a real caring for other people. The implications of such learning can be immediately explored and the outside realities of living can be made a part of the life-enhancing experiences that I consider to be an essential part of school curricula.

It is true of course that role-playing is not a new addition to education or counseling. What is new in Dr. Furness's book is an easy-to-follow manual for using role-playing procedures with a wide range of students of different ages and covering a wide range of problem situations. Thus, those of us who are reluctant to try something creative on our own have a handy guide to give us courage in exploring new ways of teaching and being in the classroom. After trying different scenarios from the book, we may feel comfortable in trying some dramatic techniques of our own. It is my hunch that the introduction of such procedures will not only make learning more fun but also more efficient, and what is even more crucial in these times of interpersonal stress, more relevant.

NORA WECKLER
Professor of Psychology
California State University, Northridge

AUTHOR'S NOTE

Regrettably, the English language does not offer a pronoun without gender, except for the frequently inappropriate "one." To fill this void, some people in recent years have advocated the use of "he/she," "s/ he," and other rather awkward locutions. In this book, we generally use the traditional male pronouns because they present less stylistic difficulty. We hope that readers will understand that "she" could be substituted for "he" in most instances in this text.

Acknowledgments

This book is dedicated to Nora Weckler who inspired me to put my ideas in book form. Everyone should have a teacher and friend like Nora!

A special bouquet of thanks to my family, George, Paulette, Hope, and Patty for their constant love and encouragement.

For their guidance, confidence, and devotion I wish to express my gratitude to my dear friends, Kathleen Conroy, Florence Rogers, Marcia Deifik, and Sue Kleinfelter.

I am also indebted to the following principals and their faculties, who over the past four years participated in testing the themes used in this book:

Jerry Langsam, Prin.
Danube St. School, Granada Hills, Ca.

Ernestine Koscza, Prin.
Knollwood School, Granada Hills, Ca.

Sonia Braverman, Director
Laurence School, Van Nuys, Ca.

Sister Marie Claudette, Prin.
Our Lady of Grace School, Encino, Ca.

Dr. Philip Smith, Director of Psych. Services Training-
    CSUN
San Cayetano School, Fillmore, Ca.

Bernice Canutt, Irene Darbyshire, Janice Farquar, Lib-
    by Ginsberg and Robert Acosta
Chatsworth High School, Chatsworth, Ca.

Diane von Buelow
St. Cyril's Junior High, Encino, Ca.

Sandra Snell
Camp Kilpatrick School, Malibu, Ca.

Frances Berger, Speech Therapist
Canejo Valley Unified School District, Thousand
    Oaks, Ca.

1

Why Role-Play?

All teachers recognize that the "problem child" can exhibit his difficulty in a variety of ways—by withdrawal, shyness, deception, showing off, insensitivity, aggression, hostility. Despite their differences, all problem children share one common trait—a poor self-concept; the child doesn't really like himself or trust himself as a person.

The timid child, feeling that whatever he does is inadequate, withdraws into the safe shell of being quiet. His fear of failure and disapproval inhibits any attempt at creative expression and communication with the outside world.

The deceptive child also is lacking in self-respect. He is afraid that if he is honest and "really me," he will not be accepted and might even be punished. He invents devious ways of coping with a world that he feels does not like him as he is.

The loud, noisy show-off is actually trying to cover up his feelings of inadequacy. His cry for attention is loud and clear.

"Everybody look at me! I can only feel worthwhile if you are paying attention to me!"

Aggressive children are often aware that their

behavior is disruptive, but it's the only way they know to fight back in a world that has denied them the love and acceptance so necessary for building a good self-concept.

But it isn't only the problem child with behavioral difficulties that suffers from a lack of self-respect. The child with a crippling disability, the child who doesn't like wearing glasses, the child with a language handicap, the culturally disadvantaged child—these children may all too easily give up and just drag along in the failure syndrome. Certainly no prescription for building self-confidence!

How can we help these children improve their image of themselves? How can we help them like and trust themselves? How can we propose alternative methods of behavior?

Mounting evidence points to the effectiveness of role-playing in realizing these goals. "A healthy self-concept is developed in the medium of reality settings rather than through mere verbalization."[1] The role-play session creates a reality setting by dramatizing situations. It is a way of "trying life on for size"

The road to an improved self-concept is through changes in behavior, feeling and expectation. Role-playing often promotes such changes. For example: a sixth grade class was acting out Role Play Situation #11, "Uh, Oh; We Smashed The Neighbor's Window!" The teacher selected the players. Raymond, a very hostile child, was selected to be the neighbor father. When the ballplayers "broke" the window, Raymond called

1. LaBenne, W. and Green, B.,*Educational Implications of Self-Concept Theory*, Pacific Palisades, Calif.: Goodyear Publishing Co., 1969, p. 123

them "stupid idiotic kids" and screamed profanities and threats at them. Raymond was apparently acting the way he thought his own father would act.

When the action was over, the teacher complimented the actors on their efforts. A class discussion followed and some of the students said that other fathers would have acted differently.

The teacher selected a second cast to enact the same situation. This time the father was extremely permissive and simply told the ballplayers to forget it.

Yet a third cast was selected. This father was kind but firm. He didn't scold or yell, but he told the boys they would have to assume responsibility for replacing the window.

The class had a lively exchange about which father they would like to have and which they thought they would be like.

How was Raymond influenced by this encounter? Several weeks later, the teacher proposed a similar role play situation (a broken gate this time). Raymond played the father and this time Raymond was like father number three.

Role-playing can sometimes effect dramatic changes in personality. Philip, an extremely withdrawn child, was chosen by this teacher to participate in a role-playing research project in California. Third grade teachers were invited to send their problem children to this center once a week for an hour. Philip's teacher had selected him because he had not spoken in class since September, and his record showed that he had been similarly silent throughout the second grade. He seemed to have no interest in other children, in play, in academics, or, for that matter, in anything. Philip's mother had eight other children and just couldn't be bothered with Philip.

The teacher conducting the role-play sessions tried every trick and gimmick he knew to try to motivate Philip to show a spark of interest, or even just to elicit from him a simple "hello." For six sessions he did not respond. At the end of the seventh session, the teacher dismissed the group but asked Philip to remain, which he did dutifully.

"Philip," he said, "we are going to put on a play and I want you to be the Indian chief. Here's the part you are to learn (a total of three lines.) You are to learn it by next week. You can have any six boys you choose to be your Indian braves."

Of course the teacher was taking a gamble at this point. There was the possibility that Philip would never show up again.

The following week Philip returned and the teacher asked him if he knew his part. He said, "no." This was the first word Philip had spoken, and the teacher was quite happy with that one word. He knew that somewhere, somehow he had touched him.

After the group was dismissed that day, the teacher again asked Philip to remain.

"Philip, if you need help, I will be glad to stay after the group leaves and help you."

Philip looked at the teacher very seriously for a few moments and then reached into his shirt pocket and pulled out the part (so he cared enough to carry the part with him.) Almost inaudibly he said, "You'd better give the part to someone else. My mother can't buy me an Indian suit."

Trying not to show his astonishment, the teacher

suggested that Philip might earn an Indian suit as a prize for the stars he collected.

After a few moments' hesitation, Philip said, "Could you help me sometime? My mother and father can't speak or read English."

That was a big step for Philip and he must have felt his teacher's enthusiasm. They practiced the lines together. When Philip left that day, there was a barely detectable little bounce to his walk.

At the next session, the teacher asked Philip to select his six Indian braves. The braves he chose were considerably taller than he was himself and included three of the brightest boys in the class. They had a short walk-through rehearsal without the dialogue. It was a mish-mash, but at least Philip was on his feet and performing.

At the actual performance, Philip, Chief Big Bear, and his braves went through their piece admirably!

Several weeks later, Philip's regular classroom teacher reported that he was raising his hand in class and offering to spell aloud.

A follow-up study made on Philip in the fourth grade, reported that his new teacher said that he was far below grade level, but seemed to be friendly, willing to try and not at all depressed.

Philip was asked what he remembered about the role-play project. "I remember that I was afraid when I first came there. But then I was the Indian chief and everybody was looking at me; and everybody clapped for me. I still play Indian chief at home and I am Big Bear and my brothers and sisters are the braves."

The role-playing situations were the only activities in Philip's school life in which he knew the feeling of success and importance. It was very significant that in this case Philip felt above even the three brightest students in the class in stature and "brightness"; and it was for the whole school to see.

It is likely that although Philip didn't take part in the role-playing in the early weeks, he may have gained insight just by being a good listener. Projecting into a role of importance may have helped Philip to discard some of his fears and reticence and gradually to develop a new self-image.

Nor are the benefits of role-playing restricted to the child with a problem. The so-called normal child also enjoys and profits from the role-play experience, in terms of improved communication skills, creativity, increased social awareness, independent thinking, verbalization of opinions, development of values and appreciation of the art of drama.

Role-play is concerned with validating the individuality of each child. When it becomes an integral part of the educational process, it can affect the child's learning powers and personality by helping him build a positive self-concept.

Through the dramatic activity involved in role-play, the child experiences alternate ways of facing situations as he acts out and plays different roles.

This medium has many advantages over traditional forms of problem solving.

1. The usual approach to problem solving is to *think* about possible solutions. Role-playing utilizes and integrates the whole person, not just his intellect. Motor, social and emotional skills are all involved simultaneously. Children who are put off by the traditional intel-

lectual academic activities are easily turned on with role-play.

2. The dramatic activity of role-play simulates the real conflicts of the child's world. Often children who find school irrelevant find role-play meaningful and involving.

3. Creative forces flow. The child in motion is operationally less anxious. His portrayal of a role is his own creation.

4. Role-play has a cathartic effect that reduces frustration and generally clears the air.

5. Many academic activities engender competitive attitudes. In role-play the atmosphere is friendly, fun-filled, relaxed, and rules of the game are readily observed.

6. Children gain insights into how the world looks from other vantage points as they are cast in different roles.

7. Too often children are learning concepts vicariously through the verbal output of adult teachers and writers. In role-play children learn by doing. Role-playing is a valuable aid to teaching because it converts ideas into direct experiences. School subjects become more realistic and thrilling when students play the roles of those they study about.

8. A much neglected area—feelings—are brought into focus.

9. As social, academic and psychological insights are gained, growth results.

10. Children become aware of the possibility of alternative choices as they observe and participate in ways other than their own of resolving problems.

11. The child not only reflects his own reality, but has a chance to role-model his hero.

12. Values are examined, defended and, possibly, changed.

13. Power moves to the child's level. Characteristically, power is administered by teacher. In the role-playing session, the children have the power to resolve and improve situations in their own way.

14. As the child interacts with his peers he strengthens, and sometimes changes his self-image.

15. In nurturing strong group identity, role-play often functions as a preventive, developmental and remedial tool.

16. Role-play is non-judgmental. There are no rights and wrongs, no correct responses or errors.

17. Role-play places a problem in the here-and-now present, where discussion deals with a past problem. The past is never as real or alive to children as the present.

2

Instructions for Getting Started

WHEN

Schedule a period for a role-play session of about ten to twenty minutes on one theme. Later, when you feel more comfortable with role-play you can initiate it spontaneously at the moment that a problem arises. For instance, if two boys come back after a recess complaining about a fight that started on the playground, it can be valuable to act out the situation while the problem is fresh. Discussion immediately following the acting out may prevent future trouble.

WHERE

Classroom or real or makeshift stage. You can use any area where voices will not be lost.

HOW

The ideal set-up is to arrange chairs in a horseshoe or circle with the stage action in the center. The teacher is part of the circular arrangement. However, for the first few sessions, the teacher and the class may feel more comfortable retaining the regular physical set-up of the room, with the "stage" at the front of the room.

Before the first session, explain to the class exactly what they will be doing. Familiarize them with the words "role-playing," "dramatic play," "acting" and "make-believe."

Ask the children to establish rules such as listening to others, trying not to interrupt, avoiding side conversations, sharing ideas with all and speaking distinctly. Explain why you are having role-play. You might say: "We are going to be actors and actresses in a real life scene. When we talk about an event, we may each have a different picture of it in our minds. If we act it out, we all have the same picture. I think you will enjoy acting out different scenes."

WHO

If asking for volunteers does not work, the teacher should select the children. Generally, children may be reluctant to volunteer but are inwardly happy to be chosen. They find that their fears that they do not know what to say or where to begin are groundless.

Never cast a shy child in the role of a shy child—make him the aggressive one. Nor should the "class cut-up" be cast in that role. It would be better for him to be cast in the role of an authority figure or someone whose behavior patterns are different from his own. The child who never succeeds should play the role of the student who wins prizes.

With a self-conscious group, it is sometimes a good idea to objectify the problem and appeal to the group for help. For instance, one of your pupils has no interest in school and refuses to do any work. As his teacher you want to motivate the child without nagging or embarrassment. Try the following:

"Children, a friend of mine who is a teacher too has a problem. Perhaps we can offer some ideas to help her solve it. She has a child who is not interested in school. He will not do his school work or his homework. What would you suggest?"

Children always enjoy solving the problems of others! Select one of their ideas to role-play. Later on they will ask what happened to the boy who doesn't like to go to school.

The most pressing question asked by teachers who are new to role-play is: "How do I get an inhibited child to participate?"

A shy child, for the purpose of this book, may be described as a child who prefers not to give a verbal response and feels more secure remaining quiet. Shyness is not necessarily suspect. The shy child may range in personality from well adjusted with a strong self-concept, to a severely withdrawn with low self-image. Shyness may be situational; the introvert in the classroom might be moderately vocal at home and extremely vocal at play.

Different cultures encourage different expressive or shyness habits in children. Mexican girls are taught to cast their eyes down when speaking, and some societies still exist where the motto "children should be seen and not heard" still prevails. A teacher who forces a child reared in a modest environment to suddenly get up and perform may be endangering that child's self-concept. This type of child will respond if allowed to move at his own pace.

Harold Greenwald, the noted psychologist-author, tells of his happy childhood, wherein he preferred losing himself in books or enjoying the company of his own thoughts to playing street games. He describes his shyness as "aloneness and pleasurable life-style."[1]

What to do about the nonparticipant and when to encourage involvement depends upon the judgment and insight of parents, teacher and child.

Sometimes a shy child will more readily participate in a mime than in a verbal role-play. With the experience he gathers in acting in mime, he may later be ready to tackle a verbal role. There are suggestions for mime lessons in this chapter and also further on in this book. (See Index, *pantomime.*)

DISCIPLINE

Yes, you will need to exercise it. Due to the relaxed structure of role-play, the atmosphere can become supercharged. Children will gain more if self-control is practiced and discipline is consistent.

If there is resistance, giggling, wisecracking, remove the instigator from the group, without anger, and with the promise that when control is gained, "we want you to come back with us."

What can the teacher do about an overactive child or a lively mischief-maker who will not allow himself to be isolated? Here are some suggestions that have been used successfully.

Try assigning a well-controlled child to work with the hyperactive one as announcers. They share the job

1. Greenwald, Harold,*Decision Therapy,*New York City, N.Y., Peter Wyden, 1973.

of announcing the names of the first cast and then stand apart from the action. When the acting is completed, they thank the boys and girls who participated, and acknowledge the courteous attention of the audience.

It will help if the teacher can involve the active child in making rules for class discipline.

Teachers have reported success in using a mischief-maker as monitor of the "Praise Board." He is responsible for recording the names of children chosen by the teacher or class for special commendation. For instance, the teacher may lead off by suggesting, "Ann, I think we all liked the way you greeted the new student. Bob, we could hear every word you said. Johnny, would you please put their names on the Praise Board?" Johnny's name can also go on the list if he has done his job well. This technique ranks high on a motivational chart and keeps Johnny on his feet. The board should remain intact until the next role-play session.

The child who finds it difficult to remain attentive often enjoys the task of tape recording the action. If he needs a helper, select one from the "quiets".

The ambitious teacher who takes his class to the auditorium and invites another class to view the role-play lesson will find that his greatest allies are the active youngsters. Their energies are expended in the lively jobs of ushering, scenery setting, lighting, timing, and returning the auditorium to its original order when the presentation is over. This does not preclude the possibility of their participating in the dramatic action; it is merely a consideration for further use of their intense energy levels.

FIRST ATTEMPTS

For the very first time a role-play session is attempted, it is sometimes helpful for the teacher to take the part of one of the players. In this way, he can avoid embarrassing silences and move the action along. Once the teacher has provided some guidelines in acting out a scene, he may step aside and let the children take over. Usually this is enough impetus and they will take off with their own ideas.

In the beginning attempts, it may sometimes happen that some children will freeze on stage and not know what to say or how to go on. If this happens before the children have really developed the theme, rather than applaud them and terminate the scene, the teacher may intercede with a specific question. This may get the children going again. In any case, the first attempts will be short.

The following lesson has been found to be very effective as an introduction to the art of role-play. It is particularly good for involving the shy child who tends to hold back from the spotlight.

Introduction   "Today, we are going to have some fun with a role-playing game called the *Magic Toyshop*. Let's pretend that we have been given our own toyshops and we can fill them with anything we please. We are going to form into six groups and each group will decide upon all the things they want in their toyshop. Each person in the group will suggest what should be in the shop and choose a job in the toyshop. Some of you may be salesmen, or you may be the toys in the shop.

"You will have about five minutes to prepare. Then I will pretend that I am a mother shopping for a birthday gift in your shops. Are there any questions?"

Some of the questions the students have asked are: "Can I have horses in my shop?" "Can I have walls lined with chocolate brownies?" "Would it be OK if I had high-heeled ladies' shoes?"

Procedure   While the children are breaking up into groups, the teacher observes the shy child. Is he slow at getting into a group? Resistant? Then select a group for him to work with. While the groups are discussing their magic toyshops, roam about, stopping to nod approval without comment. Stop beside the shy child and place your hand on his shoulder for a moment as you smile approval.

When five minutes are up, have the groups take their places and announce, "I am Mrs. Momma Galomma and I am going shopping for birthday presents for my son and daughter. Let's see, I think I'll go to this shop first.

"What do you have in this shop? (Expect some giggles.) What would you like to sell me?

"Thank you all. This is a very interesting toyshop, but I must see the others before I decide what to buy."

Repeat questions at each group. When finished, announce to all, "I have been to some very exciting toyshops today. It's difficult to choose from among all these appealing things, so I am going to buy one gift from each shop. (Teacher has been careful to note which toy the shy child represented and to choose that one.) First, I'll buy the piano from this shop. Then I'll buy the snake from this shop. Since my daughter, Bunny, likes clothes, I'll buy the high-heeled shoes from this shop. (Continue through groups.) Thanks again, children, for having such great imaginations. The next time we play this, maybe two of you can be Momma and Poppa Galomma."

Discussion   This lesson is an effective opener because it is highly motivational. The teacher is participating and the children are not put on the spot. The humorous atmosphere is a tension reducer.

The shy child will not find this activity threatening because he does not have to stand up front and be looked at. The information he shares with the group is all in fun and cannot be criticized. If he shares nothing at first, that's OK, too. No activity within the group is directed toware him individually. He is absorbed in the group dynamics and can relax and enjoy the imaginative and absurd items in the toyshops.

The teacher's hand on the shy child's shoulder is a communication of warmth and acceptance. It says "I like you." The child's self-image is given a boost when the teacher selects his toy.

The overall experience for the children has been the impression that role-playing is fun and not scary.

PANTOMIME WARM-UP

Some teachers (and children) may feel uneasy about plunging abruptly into role-play sessions. If a teacher would like to proceed more cautiously, a warm-up session, using pantomime, is a fruitful technique and gives the teacher who is inexperienced in role-play a chance to try his wings in a related activity. Pantomime is also a painless way to enlist the participation of the shy child.

The procedure is very simple. Explain that you will describe a situation and you would like some children to come up and act it out through pantomime. If there are no volunteers, choose your most outgoing pupils. Explain that no talking is necessary. For the first few attempts the teacher can take an active part in the pantomime play. If the cast calls for half-a-dozen children or more the teacher may call on the shy child to be in the cast.

If a short pantomime is produced each day the children soon get the hang of it and even the shy child will begin to volunteer. The road has been paved for role-play.

The following simple pantomime activities can be used as starters, and many easily include the shy child as a member of the cast. The situations dramatize feelings of joy, fear, anger, love, surprise, power.

1. "Today I am going to be Columbus and I'll ask some of you to be my sailors. You don't have to say a thing. Just stand beside me. See if we can make the class feel the enthusiasm of Columbus and his crew when they sighted land after spending months on the ocean with nothing but water in sight. Bob, Mary, Jane, Rita, John, will you stand beside me?"

    Teacher pantomimes walking up and down deck, looks far away, points to land, shows some excitement.

2. A group of Pilgrims and their leader meet an

Indian Chief and his braves for the first time.

3. A bully tries to cut in on the cafeteria line.

4. A child and his friends are hunting for his lost puppy.

5. A child who had moved away from town suddenly appears.

6. The Queen of Upsylvania sweeps in before her ladies-in-waiting.

7. You are practicing the violin or piano while your friends are outside playing.

8. You are at a Scout party. Your name has been drawn for a door prize, but you can't find your ticket stub.

9. You are putting on makeup for a school play when you are called to the principal's office.

10. You are at a friend's house. Your friend's mother has baked a pie and gives you a piece. You taste it. It is horrible.

11. You meet a friend in the street who has gained so much weight, you hardly recognize him.

12. Your mother gave you some money and sent you to the store for food. You are about to pay, but can't find the money.

13. You have been chosen as one of the possible winners for Halloween costume prizes. Now the judges call out the final winners one

by one. Your name is not called.

14. You are at home watching T.V. The doorbell rings. It is the postman with a package for you.

15. You and your sister go to the movies. You see two empty seats and walk down the row and sit down. Suddenly you realize that the person sitting beside you is an old friend you haven't seen for a long time.

16. You are playing in the championship baseball game. The score is tied. The bases are loaded and you are up at bat. You hit a home run.

17. You are playing outside when you discover an injured bird on the ground.

18. You are carrying a cake into the classroom. Another child bumps into you and the cake falls to the floor.

An excellent transitional activity between mime and role-play is to introduce conversation into the mimed situations.

Many of the situations were chosen for their humor. Keep the lessons light and simple; no criticism, no discussion. Try for dramatic expression. Give praise and a little applause.

SUCCESS

If you are able, in the session, merely to .get two children to stand up in front of the group, you have succeeded in getting started. They may look at you blankly and comment, "I don't know what to say." The fact that they agreed to try shows that they trust you and will involve themselves in what you have to offer. Each session brings out a little more expression of feelings. In the first few sessions, children will not know what to expect and may not want to risk making a mistake and being laughed at by the group. As the children recognize that this will not happen and that role-play is a time when they will be accepted completely, they will open up and participate more spontaneously.

3

Some Do's and Don't's

1. Budget your time. Do not allow children to go on and on aimlessly. When you see the point has been made, bring down the curtain. Often children run out of ideas and will repeat again and again what they have just said.

2. Give an assist to the dialogue when needed. For instance: In a theme such as "I'm going to ask Mom and Dad if I can keep this kitten," you may have a situation where Sue says, "Mom and Dad, can I keep this kitten?" The parents say, "No!" Dead silence follows. You suggest, "Sue, ask them why you can't keep the kitten?" Sue complies and parents respond, "It's too much mess." Sue is again lost for words. You question her, "Sue, will you take the responsibility for caring for the kitten?"

3. Encourage and praise all creative efforts. Make the children feel that whatever they have to say is important. Encourage the children to express their opinions, and always welcome their ideas whether you agree with them or not.

One of the strongest assets of the role-playing sessions is that the child who is a low achiever may receive the praise that is so vital to his self-image. He may never match the academic abilities of the better students, but in this situation he can receive equal praise and recognition. The same is true for the "naughty" boy who never has a chance to experience what it feels like to be on the other side of the fence.

Praise the efforts, rather than the person, if possible. Personal praise places a burden on the child. Psychologically, it is more valid to say, "Sue, I liked the way you spoke to Bob. We got some good ideas from that," rather than, "Sue, you were very good." Approve the action, not the child himself.

4. Give an anxious child something to hold on to—literally. A prop relieves anxiety. In almost any scene a child can be holding a book or a pad or some object.

5. Be alert to role-playing as a projective technique. A child when role-playing may be portraying a person who is at the root of his problem. The teacher may want to follow up this insight by consulting the supervisor or guidance counselor. For example, at a recent session a boy who was known to be very aggressive and hostile role-played a father as a very harsh and cruel man. The teacher discussed this with the principal who was on friendly terms with the boy. A few days later the principal called the boy to his office to give him a monitor's job. They talked about baseball and the principal brought up the subject of parents. The boy became uptight and volunteered nothing. The principal ended the interview by saying, "Bob, my door is always open to you. If you ever want to ask me anything, please feel that I am a friend, even though I must sometimes discipline you when you get into fights on the play-

ground." The principal felt he hadn't accomplished much. However, about two weeks later, Bob was at his door and a long talk followed, in which Bob got his feelings out into the open.

DON'TS

1. Never, never find fault with any dramatization no matter haw discouraged you may feel. Criticism destroys. This program cannot succeed where there is any suggestion of a critical atmosphere. Children will clam up, withdraw, and refuse to participate.
2. Don't expect instant miracles. What the children do at the beginning may not seem to be very constructive or worthwhile.

    If you have run a "tight ship" class, taking the lid off may cause a very high noise level in the beginning. It may take two or three sessions to bring about enough order so that both you and the class will benefit.
3. Don't use real names for the role-play cast. Use script names instead. Even if the children themselves suggest that they role-play a real problem they have in relation to a child, teacher or parent, use script names in place of real names.
4. Don't call for volunteers for every situation. Often the same children will volunteer and the introverts will allow them to take over. There are times when the teacher has to be more directive in order to select specific children for certain roles. Sometimes the teacher selects a stable or a gregarious child; sometimes the teacher encourages a shy child; sometimes a specific child is avoided for a specific role.

4

Sample Role-Play Session

The sample role-play session presented here took place in Mrs. DuWans' third-grade class of 24 children at Knollwood School in Granada Hills, California.

THEME

"I Got a Bad Report Card."

DURATION

Approximately 45 minutes, including the time it took the children to move their chairs into a circle.

SET-UP

Mrs. DuWans announced that there would be a class in dramatic play. She had the children bring their chairs to one corner of the room, and one by one they made a circle with the teacher as one member of the circle.

INTRODUCTION

"As soon as we are all quiet (class calms down), I'd like everyone to look sad (class giggles). Oh my, we can't look sad if we giggle. (Some gain control and try to look sad.)

"I will tell you our theme and then I would like you to think about how you would act. Here is the theme: 'I Got a Bad Report Card.' Some of you will be parents and some of you will be children.

"First, I'd like all of you to think about the child who got a bad report card. Why do you suppose this happened?"

Children's comments

Maybe the kid fooled around.

I think he didn't listen to the teacher.

She didn't do her homework.

She was absent and then she couldn't do the work.

TEACHER   Yes, these are all possible reasons. Imagine that *you* have received a bad report card—what are you going to say to your mother and father?

And, supposing you are the mother or father, how would you feel if your child whom you love comes home with a bad report card?

Sue and John, you've been listening so attentively, suppose you be Mother and Dad; and, Bryan, I like the way you were paying attention—you be Fred, the child. Do you want to think about it and talk it over? No?

All right, then I will be the teacher and we will

start the action with me giving you this folded piece of paper which is supposed to be a bad report card. (Class giggles at this because Bryan never gets a bad report card.)

PROCEDURE

TEACHER   Sorry, Fred, this is not a good report card. (Bryan [playing Fred] takes report card and, putting it behind his back, approaches Father.)

FATHER   Let me see your report card.

FRED   No.

FATHER   Why not?

FRED   It is no good.

FATHER   (*wrestles for and snatches the report card.*]What! You failed in Arithmetic and you failed in Spelling?!!? Go to your room! No television for you for a week! (Bryan obediently turns away, and father whacks him on the bottom.)

TEACHER   (starts applause to signal end.) "Well, that was very good. What did the rest of you think about that scene?"

Discussion   There followed an interesting discussion. Children noted the fact that the mother was never called upon, and that the father didn't request any explanation from his son. Neither did the son try to volunteer any excuse.

TEACHER   Who would like to do another dramatization with a different kind of mother and father and another child with a bad report card? (Hands go up.) I am delighted with your attentive participation. Before I choose another family group, does anyone have any suggestions as to how the next group might improve their presentation?

Children's comments:

> Speak louder.
>
> Be more serious.
>
> Plan ahead of time.

TEACHER   Very good. This time Sue will choose a mother; John, you choose a father; and Bryan, you choose a child. (They select.) Fine, you three go to a corner and plan your action. Meanwhile we here in the circle will choose groups for another theme, "I Got a Good Report Card."

Intermission   At this point there were classroom interruptions—boys had to take milk cartons out and a teacher's aide came into the room and joined the circle. The children became a little noisy and the teacher called for quiet by saying, "Some of us have been waiting patiently so we will go on now. I will ask Marla to be Anita, the child with a good report card." (Marla is a very withdrawn child and an underachiever who has never known the feeling of being successful in school.) Ronald, you be her father, and Patty, you be the mother. Would you like to go to the corner and plan?"

By this time, the second bad report card group was ready and re-entered the circle to set up their scene. The good report card scene was shelved for the moment.

PROCEDURE

TEACHER   Jill, I am sorry, but this report card is not good. (Alice [playing Jill] takes card and goes to mother.)

JILL   Mother, you aren't going to like this. (Hands the report card to mother. Mother looks it over.)

MOTHER   Well, it looks like you will have to study more. I can help you with Spelling and Reading. We will have to work together. (Hands card to father.)

FATHER   Hmmm, what's this I see? Goofing off again! Did you try your best?

JILL   Yes, I did the best I could.

FATHER   Well, if you did the best you could, okay. But you'd better buckle down, or else!

JILL   I will try harder, Dad.

Discussion   The teacher started the applause at this point. A lively discussion followed concerning the two sets of parents. Some children expressed surprise at the fact that the second child with a bad report card didn't get a spanking or any other form of punishment. Others defended the second troupe of role players and explained that their parents, like the second set of parents, would look forward to a better report card by providing help at home.

The teacher offered the comment that each child is responsible for motivating himself to achieve a better report.

One child noted that he had attended a school where they didn't get report cards. An interesting exchange of ideas followed this.

The "good report card" group was now ready.

TEACHER (TO MARLA)   Well, Anita, I am happy to tell you that you have earned all A's. How do you feel? (Marla looks skeptically at the teacher and doesn't answer. The teacher repeats what he said.)

After a long silence, Marla says, "Good." (She takes the card, turns to her parents and without a word hands it to the mother.)

MOTHER   Oh, look at this. All A's! This is much better than your last report card. Oh, Anita, I am so proud of you. Aren't you proud of her, honey? (At the word "honey," the class roars and the father blushes. The teacher demands silence by saying, "Let's be real people.")

FATHER   Let's see this report card. Yes, it is real good. Shall we get her a present?

MOTHER   Yes! What would you like, Anita? (Marla doesn't respond. This is a new role for her and she can't quite handle it.)

MOTHER   Don't you want anything?

ANITA   No.

Teacher ends action with applause.
Marla's feelings are gently drawn out. The teacher

asks Marla, "How did you feel bringing home that report card, Marla? Were you excited when a reward or present was suggested?" Marla finally declares softly that a good report card is enough of a present for her.

The class complains that they couldn't hear Marla.

TEACHER   Marla, you were doing such a good job of being the girl with the good report card that you probably forgot about your voice. Next time I know you will remember to speak louder.

The session comes to a close and the teacher winds up the period with:

"Who didn't have a chance to act today? (Hands go up.) Next time you people will be first. Now, we have a visitor who came to watch us. Suppose we tell her how we feel about dramatic play."

Children's comments:

It is fun to do.

I like making believe I am somebody else.

I wish we could make up our own themes.

I wish Gary wouldn't giggle so much.

I'd like to do this every day.

TEACHER   We are finished now. One by one please take your chairs quietly back to your tables.

Discussion   Not once was any child so disorderly that he disrupted the entire activity. Had this happened,

Mrs. DuWans would have sent the child back to his place at his table and given him seat work. This action would reinforce the rules of the circle.

Mrs. DuWans used praise wherever possible. There was never a criticism, and if a criticism came from the audience, she used it constructively to point out a praiseworthy idea. The class was very much at ease and very unselfconscious. They seemed to be very happy, and completely involved in what they were doing. The teacher's positive attitude reinforced the enthusiasm and success of the role-playing session.

5

52 LESSON PLANS

This chapter consists of 52 lesson plans for role-playing. Each lesson plan lists the specific aims for the topic, procedures for implementing the role-play, and suggestions about some of the major points that should emerge in the discussion following the role-play.

Lesson Plan 1
"THERE'S A NEW STUDENT IN OUR CLASS"

Aims To share experiences of having been in new or unfamiliar situations.

To discuss ways to make a new child feel welcome.

To develop empathy for another person who feels like an outsider.

To help children express any feelings they may have of aloneness and isolation.

The assumption is that the teacher has previously explained what role-play is, and that the class may have done some pantomime warm-ups. If not, then role-play will have to be explained first.

Introduction   "Children, today we are going to try role-playing. I will give you a situation and you will be the actors and actresses. This is the situation: Pretend a new student has joined our class today. Now it is play time. You are all out on the playground. Two of you are playing a game and you notice the new student standing alone. What would you say or do?"

Procedure   Teacher asks for volunteers or chooses two children to play a game, and one child to be the new classmate. When these children are in their places, give them a start signal and let the action evolve. Stop the dramatization (by beginning the applause) when it has more or less made its point.

Discussion   "That was very good. How do you think the new child felt at first? How did the newcomer feel about being invited to join the game?

"Does anyone have another idea of how to greet a new classmate? Let's try the same scene with three different actors. This time, we will pretend it's lunchtime and everybody is in the cafeteria.

"Before we begin, does anyone want to make any comments or suggestions? Could you all see and hear the actors well enough?"

Proceed with second role-play as with first.

Older children may want to compare the second role-play with the first. Younger children, depending upon the group, may find comparisons beyond their comprehension and confusing. Always begin comparisons with "What was good about what the actors did?" This eases the criticism that may follow. One problem with comparisons is that they invite the concept that one action is better then another. This can damage the free and open atmosphere you hope to create. The important thing about multiple productions is that they demonstrate that there are alternative ways of reacting.

Lesson Plan 2
"OUR FIELD TRIP IS CANCELLED"

Aims   To explore alternative ways of handling feelings of disappointment.
To express and observe reactions in a very frustrating situation.

Introduction   "Class, we are going to make believe that we are all going on a field trip to the museum. We have money for souvenirs, delicious box lunches, and the air is full of happy anticipation. We get on the bus, take our seats and are ready to go.

"Bill, you come up and be the bus driver. Take a chair and put it where you think the bus driver would be. Mary, you are the class leader for the trip. I'd suggest you sit directly behind Bill. The rest of you imagine you are seated on the bus."

The theme is not announced in advance. The teacher takes the bus driver aside and tells him, "Bill, the bus is going to be fine for one block or so and then it will break down. If you like, you can get out of the bus and tinker around and try to get it fixed. Then you have to tell the class leader that the trip will have to be cancelled and she will announce this to the class."

Procedure   Two chairs are placed up front for the

driver and the class leader. The other students, while involved in the role-play, remain in their seats but pretend to be on the bus. The teacher is on the bus too.

When the leader announces that the trip is cancelled, the teacher encourages the class to react to the situation. (e.g. "How do you all feel about not being able to go to the museum as planned?") It will be interesting to see the different types of responses.

Action should not go over three minutes, at which time the teacher raises his hand and says "cut." If the teacher prefers, he may have a student act as timekeeper and stop the action after a given time period.

The role-play may be repeated with a new driver and a new leader. Of course, this time the situation will not come as a surprise. But it will be interesting to note whether any of the children have altered their attitudes from the first role-play to the second.

Discussion   "Children, that was a very great disappointment to all of us, wasn't it? Have any of you been in a situation when you were frustrated? How did you react when things didn't go the way you planned?

"What are some things we can do when we are faced with disappointment?

"Do you suppose there is anyone who never knew disappointment?

"Is it important to learn how to handle frustration? Some wise man once said, 'when life gives you lemons, make lemonade.' What did he mean by that?"

Lesson Plan 3
"WE'RE LOST."

Aims To confront the problem of fear.

To elicit responses of resourcefulness and courage in a situation of possible danger.

Introduction "Imagine yourselves in the following situation. Four of you have been having a picnic in a park you've never been to before. You have had fun playing games and now you are eating. You are talking about the fun you've had when one of you remarks that it is getting dark and maybe it's time to go home. Suddenly you all realize that no one knows the way home. How would you act in this situation?"

Procedure The teacher may choose the four pupils to act out this situation. This way, he can arrange to have three fairly confident, outgoing children and one somewhat shy child.

    Actors take their places on stage and get involved in the action. Try to limit the play to about three minutes, but allow the action to be completed. Then the class as a whole may discuss the role-play. Or, the class may be broken up into small groups to discuss what they saw and make their own suggestions for what they would do. Each group may then take its turn to role-play.

Discussion This is a very successful vehicle for the shy child who has been reluctant to participate. It is a means of getting the child up on stage to be part of a group situation even if he doesn't participate in the talk. Don't be discouraged if the shy child just stands there looking uncomfortable. Although he may appear to be embarrassed, often you will later discover that he has actually been pleased with himself.

Under no circumstances, however, force a child to participate if he doesn't really want to. Do not even ask him why he won't take part; when he is ready, he will.

Lesson Plan 4
"WOWIE, I'M GOIN' TO HAVE A GREAT TIME."

Aims   To note how the child makes choices about whom he wants to share his joy with.

To act out a fantasy wish-fulfilling situation.

To explore the implications of choosing one or two friends (out of a whole class) for a special treat.

Introduction   "Today we are going to pretend that your uncle has phoned you long distance. He has invited you to visit him for two weeks. You can bring any two friends you choose. He will send you the airplane tickets, and he promises to take you to all the most exciting places."

Procedure   "Let's have one volunteer. We will start the scene with the phone ringing. How would you act if this happened to you? What would you do as soon as you hung up the phone?"

Discussion   After a few comments such as, "That sure sounds thrilling! What an exciting happening!" the teacher may ask those chosen, "How did you feel when Charles invited you to go along with him?"

After the happy feelings have been expressed, the teacher may choose to explore the feelings of the unchosen. "Who would like to share with us his feelings about not having been chosen to share this marvelous opportunity?"

"Do you find that as you grow older you are better able to accept the fact that you are not always chosen?"

It has been shown that one of the reasons youngsters turn to drugs and alcohol is that as children they didn't learn to handle disappointment.

Lesson Plan 5
"WHY WASN'T I INVITED TO THE PARTY?"

Aims   To imagine what it feels like to be rejected.

To promote an exchange about similar experiences.

To explore tactful ways of inviting some friends to a party without hurting others.

Introduction   "I am going to ask one of you to pretend you are planning a party. I will ask four of your classmates to come on stage and you will invite all but one of them to the party. Here are three pieces of paper to use as make-believe invitations.

Jeanette, come up and be the party girl.

Al, Amy, Sam and Marie, you will be the friends. Amy, you will be the one who is not invited."

Procedure   In choosing the child to be rejected, the teacher should select one who is popular and is always invited to parties.

This situation lends itself well to role reversal. When the first acting out is over, do a second one with the rejected child doing the inviting this time. The rest of the cast may be changed.

Discussion   This is a good situation to use before holiday times when children will be giving and getting Valentine's Day cards, Christmas cards, party invitations, and some will be left out.

Sidney Jourard[1] writes about the value of sharing one's own experiences with others as one of the most effective ways to build trust. If a teacher shares with his class an experience of living through the sadness of not having been invited to a special party, the children feel that the teacher understands how they feel when they are rejected because he had the same experience. To be understood is one of the greatest gifts a child can receive.

Start the discussion following the role-play by relating a personal experience, telling exactly how you felt. Don't be afraid to report your emotions if you

1. Jourard, Sidney M., *The Transparent Self: Self-Disclosure and Well Being*, New York, N.Y., Van Nostrand Reinhold Co., 1971.

were angry, bitter, resentful or revengeful. Children respect honesty. They will be anxious to hear how you overcame your frustration.

"I have told you my story, and I wonder if you, Amy, felt somewhat the same. Did you feel lonely and unwanted?"

"Has anyone in this class ever had to face a similar situation?

"Often we can't invite everyone in the class to a party. What can we do to make those who are not invited feel we still like them and don't wish to hurt their feelings?"

Lesson Play 6
"I HAVE TO GO TO THE HOSPITAL."

Aims   To relieve anxiety and fear about the hospital ordeal.

To share a frightening experience.

To regard the experience as an adventure.

To appreciate the positive aspects of a painful situation.

Introduction   "Class, today we are going to role-play the theme, 'I have to go to the hospital.' Many of you have been to a hospital so this theme is familiar."

We need a doctor, a nurse, a receptionist, a mother and father, and maybe a few visitors.

"Johnny is going to the hospital soon. If you'd prefer, you can just watch and see what goes on in a hospital."

Procedure   Children can use a desk for the receptionist, chairs for a hospital bed, and props for instruments. If the children would like, they can costume themselves. Action can take three minutes.

Discussion   "Thank you, boys and girls. That was a fine presentation. Maybe some of you who have been in a hospital can tell us what was true in this scene. How was it like or different from your real experience in the hospital?

"Some of the time we spend in the hospital is painful, but some of the time is very pleasant. What may make it pleasant?"

Children generally love this scene. It is one of the best sessions for a teacher who has never tried role-playing. The atmosphere is fun and light-hearted. Johnny's anxiety is, in part, alleviated by hearing from children who have gone through the experience with no ill effects. He may realize that there are some good things to be said for his forthcoming ordeal.

Lesson Plan 7
"I GOT A BAD REPORT CARD / I GOT A GREAT REPORT CARD."

Aims   To give the child who has only known failure an experience of what it's like to feel success.

To enable the child to see himself in relation to his parents.

To illustrate that adults may react differently to the same situation.

Introduction   "Today we are going to have some of you pretend to be parents while others pretend they are their children. Let's have Bob be the father, and Nora, you be the mother. Kate, you will be the child and you will make believe you got a very bad report card."

Procedure   Mom and Dad stand next to each other on stage and Kate walks up to them with the report card in hand. Select a student who always gets a good report card to play the child with the bad report card.

Following this action, select a child who never gets a good report card to come home to Mom and Dad with a great report card.

Both role-play situations may be repeated with different casts before the discussion starts.

Discussion   It will be very interesting to observe how different children portray the parents' reaction to the bad report card.

The child who fails in school sometimes gives the teacher interesting clues as to his family background when he is asked to play the parent role.

Lesson Plan 8
"I WANT MY SWEATER BACK."

Aims   To explore ways of dealing with feelings of frustration and anger.

To promote a discussion about respecting the property rights of others.

To examine what's involved in standing your ground, especially against someone you're afraid of.

Introduction   "The pretend situation for today is this: You have lost your new sweater somewhere in school and it has your name on it. You are looking for it when along comes a much older boy who is known to be pretty rough. He is carrying your sweater. How are you going to get it back?"

Procedure   Use a sweater and call for volunteers for the two parts. Stop the action when it becomes physical or repetitious. Then try it again with different actors.

Discussion   This is an excellent situation for both aggressive and withdrawn children to become involved in—in both roles.

Make it clear to the class that the younger boy's name is in the sweater.

Expect many different reactions .One child may handle this problem by trying to grab the sweater back. Another child may try talking the older boy into giving it up. Another child may threaten to report the older boy if he refuses to give up the sweater.

One boy came up with the following solution. He decided to "play it cool" to get his sweater back. He did not confront the other boy. He found the boy's name and had his parents contact the school principal who handled the problem without revealing that the parents had called.

The initial class reaction to the above solution was, "Sissy, he had to run to Mommy," but after discussion of the consequences of other actions, the children changed their minds. They agreed that this solution was good because the boy got his sweater back without confronting the bully and risking a possible beating.

The teacher can lead into the problem of dealing with a bully by questions such as: Which presentation do you think will bring about the result we want, which is to get the sweater back, with as little trouble as possible? If fighting and arguing with a bully are fruitless, then should you get someone older to help solve the problem?

What persons in authority might be willing to help us?

The discussion can also deal with ways of protecting your own property, respecting the property of others, and avoiding the pitfalls of leaving things where someone might be tempted to take them. It is a valuable opportunity to explain the role of the authority figures such as the policeman, school principal, counselor and others who are there to help and protect us.

Lesson Plan 9
"THEY CALLED ME NAMES."

Aims   To experience what it feels like to be made fun of.

To discuss feelings of embarrassment, humiliation, hurt, anger, resentment.

To promote tolerance for individual differences.

To examine the phenomenon of scapegoating.

To elicit positive and constructive suggestions for dealing with such situations.

Introduction   "I would like Ken to come up and play a special role today—the role of Fatso Doolan. I would also like two volunteers. Your roles will be to follow Fatso on his way to school and taunt him about being fat."

Procedure   Select a child for Fatso who is neither fat nor the object of any taunts. If he can stuff something inside his shirt to make himself look fat, it will keep the session from getting too serious or hostile.

Action should take no more than two minutes.

Discussion   "Thank you, children. Is there anyone in this class who has never been made fun of?

"How do you think Fatso felt?

"Have any of you had similar feelings because you were teased about something that made you feel bad?

"What did you do about it?

"What can we do about people who humiliate us?

"Let's take a look at the scapegoater. What do you think causes a person to make fun of someone? Do you think they are unaware that it will hurt the other person?

"Is it possible that it makes the teaser feel like a big shot? Is it possible that this is the only way that he can build himself up to feel equal to others?

"Do you think that deep inside, a person who is a teaser does not feel good about himself for some reason that we don't know about? Do you think that we should feel sorry for the teaser?

"Is it possible that giving a hurtful teaser some praise about his good qualities would help?

"This is a big order, but I wonder how some of you feel about helping and coping with this problem."

Variations on this theme can focus on other features children are sensitive about, such as nicknames, skin problems, eyeglasses, and physical defects.

Lesson Plan 10
"CHIRPY THE CHEATER DID IT AGAIN."

Aims   To give a child who resorts to cheating a chance to hear without embarrassment how his classmates view his behavior.

To reflect on the positive and rewarding feelings of being trusted by others.

To probe into underlying reasons for behavior.

Introduction   "Children, I have brought a friend to join our class for the role-playing session today. His name is Chirpy the Cheater. Chirpy is a very nice little boy, but he has been known to sometimes cheat in the classroom. Let's make believe that Chirpy cheated on a test and all of you know it. I didn't see him, so I am not sure about it. Let's pretend that I have just left the room. I'd like you to come up one by one and say something to Chirpy. Speak loud enough so that we can hear what you say."

Procedure   Chirpy the Cheater is a male or female doll dressed to look like a student. Chirpy is placed in an empty chair in the middle of the stage. We don't use a child to play Chirpy for obvious reasons. Using a doll gets the idea across without damaging or threatening anyone.

Teacher proceeds around the room inviting any child who wants to, to come up and address Chirpy.

Discussion   Hopefully the children did more than express their negative reactions. If not, the teacher might ask them to think about why Chirpy would cheat. This might not only throw light on possible motivation, but may elicit reassurance from the children, as well as suggestions for changing.

Lesson Plan 11
"UH OH, WE SMASHED THE NEIGHBOR'S WINDOW."

Aims   To explore different solutions to a problem in which you are faced with a conflict between fear of punishment and respect for the rights of others.

To give children a chance to put themselves in the position of the offended as well as the offender.

Introduction   "In our scene today, some children are playing outdoors. Two of the children are playing baseball. One of them hits a ball that smashes a neighbor's window. Who would like to be the boy who hits the ball, and who would like to be the people who live in the house?"

Procedure   Use one side of the stage as a play area where several children are playing. The boys playing ball are at opposite ends of the stage. The family next door is in back of the boy who missed the catch.

Repeat this scene with several different casts.

Discussion   After all the action is completed, the class discusses the different presentations. Have the class vote on the best solution for what to do about the broken window. Have the children reenact the most favored script.

Lesson Plan 12
"MY TEACHER SENT ME TO THE PRINCIPAL'S OFFICE."

Aims   To give children a chance to share their feelings about a common experience.

To give insight into the feelings of the adult who is the authority figure.

Introduction   "Does the title of our role-playing session for today sound familiar? How many of you have had to go to the principal's office for some reason or other? Let's role-play the scene that caused you to go. Who can tell us of a trip that you made to the principal's office?"

Procedure   As hands go up, call on children to relate their experiences. Continue until you have had a variety of experiences, including some in which the child was joyful, fearful or wondering. Then select a few different scenes for dramatization. Start with a happy situation, then a wondering one, finally a frightening one. Have children reverse roles, so that a boy or girl sent to the principal can also feel what it must be like to be the principal.

Discussion   "Thank you, children. How did you feel being the principal?

"Were you aware that the principal has to make many different decisions in one day?

"What is the nicest part of the principal's job?

"Is there anything we can do to make his task easier?"

This theme can be applied to other adult figures in authority such as doctor, dentist, religious leader, therapist, and so on.

Lesson Plan 13
"HENRY'S GRANDFATHER DIED AND I JUST DON'T KNOW WHAT TO SAY."

Aims   To alleviate the embarrassment of not knowing what to say when a relative of a classmate dies.

To help the bereaved understand that children may be caring, but not know how to express it.

To help children become aware that positive feelings that remain unexpressed lose their value, and that ignoring the situation may be almost as bad as saying the wrong thing.

Introduction   "Children, our theme for role-playing today is: 'Henry's grandfather died and I just don't know what to say.' Have any of you ever been in this situation? I know I have. Perhaps in acting this out, we can figure out some comforting things to say."

Procedure   "Now, for this scene I'll ask Celia to be our mourner. She is walking home from school and feeling very sad. She meets Norma, Alice, Bill and Jane, one at a time. Try to be natural and just do whatever you would under these circumstances."

There are three concepts which the teacher may offer the children to help them express the generous response which is present in the heart but sometimes can't seep out. The teacher may write these on the board before the scene, or she may begin with the role-play and write them up after the action. Some children benefit from rehearsing the responses beforehand, while other children need to be in the situation first.

The key procedures found most helpful to put the mourner at ease are:

1. Offer to do something! "Is there anything I can do to help?"

2. Talk about the dead person! "I met him . . ."

3. Share your own sad time! "I know how you feel. My favorite uncle died . . ."

The role-play action can be repeated, casting different actors in the roles. Practice with a variety of verbal expressions and repetition are all-important.

Discussion "Did it seem awkward to use one of the phrases from the board? That is natural, but when a real occasion occurs, you'll be happy to have helpers like these key phrases.

"Why are we embarrassed when we meet someone who has lost a loved one?"

"Is the mourner also embarrassed?

"What can happen if we don't communicate our feelings to the other person? How will they know we care?"

This theme was suggested by an eleven-year-old boy whose father died. He was so upset by what the children in his class said to him that he refused to go to school. The teacher's inquiry revealed that the children had meant to comfort Allen, but didn't know how. They modeled their responses to Allen's grief on data they had gathered from watching television. Such remarks as "Tell me all the gory details," were typical. Well-meaning, perhaps, but shattering to Allen.

A question that is often probed by children is: "What if Henry didn't like his grandfather, then what?" Key Phrase #1 is appropriate in every circumstance surrounding death. It is honest and solicits an honest response. Children can readily appreciate that whether Henry liked his grandfather or not, he is sad at his death. Even if his sadness is mixed with guilt, he needs comforting.

Lesson Plan 14
"MY CLASS IS NOISY AND MY CHILDREN KEEP INTERRUPTING ME."

Aims   To give children the feel of trying on the role of teacher.

To have children appreciate how frustrating their behavior may sometimes be.

To elicit children's ideas of appropriate disciplinary measures.

To give the withdrawn child a chance to misbehave.

Introduction   "Today you are going to imagine you are a teacher who is constantly interrupted with loud voices, funny noises, or questions that have no meaning to the lesson. I will be an interrupting student today. Let's see what it would be like if you were the teacher in this situation."

Procedure   Select a child to give a spelling quiz. (If you have had children teach spelling lessons before and they are prepared for this, it makes for a more interesting scene.) For the first role-play, the teacher should be the interrupter. After this, the teacher should select the withdrawn children to be the interrupters.

Discussion   It should be interesting to see how the children role-playing teacher portray this role.

Lesson Plan 15

"I ALWAYS GET BLAMED FOR WHAT MY BROTHER DOES."

Aims   To elicit ideas for positive ways of handling negative situations.

To help the victim of unfair blame feel less isolated by showing it is a common problem.

Introduction   "Children, have you ever heard someone say, 'I always get blamed for what my brother did?' Do you know anyone who always seems to get blamed? Today, I am going to ask you to tell us about a time when a person you know had to take the blame and suffer for what someone else did. Please tell what happened and what your friend did about it."

Procedure   Allow time for children to tell about these experiences. Then select a few situations that can be turned into role-play scenes. You can let the child who told the story be the director of the role-play and choose people to play the different parts. However, make sure that make-believe names are assigned to the characters.

Discussion   "Thank you, children. It looks like getting blamed for what someone else did is a universal problem, and happens to children all over.

"Would it help if we tried to understand what causes unfair blame? Is it that grown-ups are in a hurry to settle a problem and sometimes take the quickest solution? What other reasons can you suggest?

"I'd like to tell you a story about Ellen, who was in the class of a teacher who is a friend of mine. Ellen was required to take care of her little sister, Poogee, whenever Mother went out to the neighbor's house or shopping. As soon as the mother would leave, little sister Poogee would tear through the house, often damaging things. Ellen became so frustrated, she locked little sister in the bedroom. When the mother returned, Poogee was screaming, the house was in disarray and guess who was blamed?

"Ellen understood her mother's anger, but did not want to take the blame any longer. This is how Ellen solved her problem. Instead of sulking, she waited until things were peaceful and her mother was alone. She said to her mother: 'Mom, I would like to ask your advice about something. There's a problem I want to talk about. If you have time now or tomorrow, it would be great.'

"Her mother said that now was as good a time as any and Ellen began, 'Mom, I want to help you with Poogee but it is awful. I just can't control her and I don't like to be blamed for things that are not my fault. It makes me feel like hitting her, or crying because I'm so mad. It's not fair. What do you think, Mom?'

"Ellen's mother was surprised at Ellen's approach. She thought it over and things did improve at Ellen's house.

"What made Ellen's way of solving her problem better than sulking or trying to get even with Poogee?

"Do you think that Ellen's mother had not really thought about it from Ellen's viewpoint before? Do you think it helps to tell people how we feel about things?"

Lesson Plan 16

"I ALWAYS HAVE TO TAKE CARE OF MY BABY SISTER WHEN THE OTHER KIDS ARE OUT PLAYING."

Aims   To identify the feelings of different members of the family in a conflict situation.

To promote a discussion of possible attitudes and solutions to a realistic problem.

Introduction   "Children, today the scene involves a big brother and his baby sister. The boy's friends knock on the door and ask him to join them in a ball game. He asks his mother who says, 'No, you have to take care of your baby sister.' How are they going to solve this problem?"

Procedure   Select a child who is respected by his peers to role-play the big brother. Since no attention is directly on brother's friends, try selecting a shy student for this role. Select a popular child for the mother role.

Discussion   This is a familiar experience to many children and will elicit strong feelings. The scene should be reenacted with different casts to demonstrate various possible problem-solving techniques. Comments and suggestions should be elicited from the children both in response to the dramatizations and from their own experience. It will be interesting to see whether some of the techniques from previous role-play sessions have begun to be incorporated.

Lesson Plan 17
"NOBODY WANTS TO PLAY WITH ME."

Aims To open discussion on how to win friends.

To help a rejected child try to understand how he himself might be contributing to his own rejection.

To gain insight into how it feels to be rejected, and to experience what it's like to be rejecting.

Introduction "Class, today's role-playing session concerns a boy who wants to join the groups at school but nobody wants to play with him. Let's role-play this scene and then talk about how the boy feels being an outsider. What suggestions can we give him so that he may be accepted by the others and welcomed into their games?"

Procedure Choose one of the most popular children in the class to play the rejected child. Have three groups of two and three children scattered on stage busy with games. When the action is called, the outsider will try to join each group in their play. Each in turn rejects him.

Discussion This is a very broad and universal problem with children. A question that should dominate the session would be: What do I have to do to make friends?

Lesson Plan 18
"MY MOTHER DOESN'T LIKE MY FRIENDS."

Aims   To air different viewpoints.

To try to project into both the child's and the mother's points of view.

To foster creativity through group participation and dynamics.

Introduction   "Today we are going to do something a little different with our role-play session. You are to form into groups of five or six. For this session, please choose to join children who are not your close friends. It's also a good idea for each group to have both boys and girls.

"When you have formed into groups, I will give you a problem situation and I would like each group to create a play that they will act for us.

"The problem is: 'My mother doesn't like my friends.'"

Procedure   Give the children a little time to organize themselves into groups and to plan their scene. Move about among the groups to see if they are making headway. If a group has bogged down, you might suggest that they choose one member to be chairman. A few questions might be helpful. (e.g. What role are you playing? Who is the mother? Where and when does youc scene take place?)

Discussion   After all the presentations are over, allow class time for free comment, questions, suggestions. The variety of approaches usually kicks off lively discussion. You may want to choose a recorder to keep track of all the ideas generated.

Lesson Plan 19
"HE ALWAYS PUSHES AND HITS EVERYONE WHEN THE TEACHER ISN'T LOOKING."

Aims   To help children appreciate the effect of their behavior on their classmates.

To illustrate that disagreeable behavior makes a child unpopular with his peers.

To gain insight into why a child may be using inappropriate means to gain attention.

To find agreeable solutions to help a child overcome his impulsive behavior.

Introduction   "Children, in our role-play scene for today a few of you are standing in line and a boy or girl tries to get up ahead by pushing someone else out of the line. The teacher doesn't see what happened."

Procedure   For this session, choose a child who does push and hit others to be the first in the line so that he will see what it feels like to be pushed. Stop the action as soon as the pushing takes place.

Discussion   "How did it feel to be pushed and hit?

"How do the rest of you feel about someone who hits and pushes others?

"How can we handle these situations?"

Lesson Plan 20
"I'M AFRAID TO RAISE MY HAND SO I NEVER DO AND I JUST KEEP QUIET."

Aims   To help children feel secure about communicating their ideas to others.

To encourage children to participate in group activities.

To enable a timid or apathetic child to get an objective view of himself and see the impact of his withdrawal on others.

Introduction   "Children, in our role-play session today, I am going to play the part of the student. Make believe that all of you are teachers and I am your student. You may one by one ask me a question about any subject. You may quiz me in spelling, arithmetic, social studies or any other school subject. Or, if you'd rather ask about my hobbies or likes and dislikes, you may do so."

Procedure   Give each child a chance to ask a question. The teacher replies to each question inaudibly and in garbled tones or monosyllables. The children will respond at first by giggling, but soon their amusement will turn to irritation. Stay with it until you reach this point! Action is stopped when there are no more questions.

Discussion "What is it like when you ask someone a question and you get a response you can't hear or understand? Do you have any idea of why I would answer in this way?

"Would it have been better if I had given a wrong answer instead of mumbling something I didn't want you to hear?

"How do you feel when you can't communicate with someone?

"How do you feel about a classmate who doesn't talk to you? How can we help such a student feel that whatever he says is worthwhile, even if the answer is wrong?"

Sometimes the children will point out that someone in the class is like the person in this scene. The teacher should quickly lead the discussion away from individuals. He might point out that the problems used in role-playing are universal and are shared by many people, and that in role-play we become aware of how the things we do, whatever they are, affect others. The problem of being shy is a very common one. The teacher might share a personal experience of his own about a time when he felt scared to participate.

Lesson Plan 21
"BARRY IS SAYING THINGS ABOUT ME THAT AREN'T TRUE."

Aims   To help children accept responsibility for what they say about others.

To help children understand that gossip can be destructive.

To help children become aware of the value of keeping a friend's secret.

To discuss the meaning of trust.

Introduction   "Class, today the theme of our session is 'Barry is telling stories about me that aren't true.' Would someone volunteer to be Barry? I need four people to come up and just stand by chatting away about anything. We will pretend that one of the four is named Jim. Barry will come along and join the group. He will tell the group that Jim's teacher sent him to the auditorium to set up chairs for the assembly program, but because Jim is so lazy he chickened out and went to the Nurse's office instead, making believe he had a stomach ache.

"Jim will protest, and the rest of the group will question both Jim and Barry to try to determine if this is truth or gossip."

Procedure   If no one volunteers to be Barry, the teacher will select someone or play the role himself. Select a child who is well liked to be Barry.

Discussion   "Class, how do you feel about what Barry did?

"Why do people gossip?

"Does it matter whether what they say is true or not? What is the effect on the subject of the accusation?

"How can we check ourselves when we feel tempted to say something that would hurt another person?"

Avoid role-playing a situation like this, which elicits strong feelings, on the same day that the situation has arisen as a reality in the classroom.

Lesson Plan 22
"YOU'RE A NO-GOOD CHEAT AND I'M SO MAD AT YOU I'M GONNA PUNCH YOU IN THE FACE."

Aims   To find appropriate techniques for handling violent reactions to a frustrating experience.

To encourage children to try constructive ways of settling differences.

To see the futility of getting angry about minor mishaps.

To develop a sense of perspective about whether the reaction is appropriate to the cause.

To experience the positive feelings that follow "clearing the air."

Introduction   "Children, today we are going to role-play a scene in which two teams are playing baseball. A fight breaks out because a player on one team insists that his stolen base is safe. The argument gets so heated that it results in insults and name-calling."

Procedure   Start the action with the pitcher throwing to the batter and the man already on first ready to steal to second base. Four for each team is sufficient to get the point across. The scene can be enacted first with an all girls' team and then with an all boys' team. Stop the action before it gets out of hand.

Discussion   "You have all seen what can happen when we become so angry that our feelings overtake our power to settle a fight in a constructive manner. This kind of fighting can destroy our relationships with other people, whether they are close friends, class-mates, brothers and sisters, or parents. Arguments are healthy if we argue in a fair and just manner. How do we do that? I will write a three-step method called "Fight Fair" on the board:"

1. *State the facts as calmly as possible.*Only the here-and-now-facts count.

Never refer to anything in the past, or make predictions about the future. (Example: State, "I slid into base before you tagged me out." Avoid, "You always...." or "Last time we played you...." statements.)

2. *Express how you feel.*

Talk about your own feelings. Avoid making negative statements about the other person's character.

(Example: "I feel very angry when you call me names. I don't like that.")

3. *Find out what you can do about the situation.*

If you are careful not criticize or blame each other, you can demonstrate that you are willing to cooperate in a solution to the problem. (Example: "Have you any ideas about how we can settle this so we can still be friendly?")

Try the same scene again using the "Fight Fair" method. Discuss it. It's easy, but it works wonders most of the time.

NOTE   The "Fight Fair" method is an outgrowth of the principles laid down by George R. Bach and Peter Wyden in their book, *The Intimate Enemy,* New York, William Morrow & Co., 1969. Although the book is written for adults, the rules prescribed for how to have a well-trained fight apply to children as well.

Children who understand the "three steps" will have an excellent tool to guide them in one of the most important phases of all interpersonal relationships: fighting.

In the next lesson plan, the same principles are used in a child-parent fight scene.

Lesson Plan 23
"I BUMPED AGAINST THE LAMP AND BROKE IT."

Aims   To help children use the "three step Fight Fair

method" in confronting a parent in an explosive situation.

To suggest that confrontation is better than avoidance in handling problems.

To illustrate that honest, direct handling of a situation results in trust, while dishonesty or failure to face up to problems causes mistrust.

To promote self-respect and build good self images.

Introduction   "Class, our role-play scene for today will give us practice in using the Fight Fair method in facing an unpleasant task. Can someone tell us what the three steps of the Fight Fair method are?

"Listen closely to the theme and try to imagine how you might use the three-step method in this situation. The theme is: 'Mom, while you were out shopping, Susie and I were kidding around and I bumped against the lamp and broke it'."

Procedure   "We can use a plastic bottle for a lamp. Two of you are involved in horseplay and wham, the lamp crashes to the floor. You are both upset and you are picking up the pieces when mother walks in. Any volunteers? Action!"

Teacher may have to guide the children in using the Fight Fair steps if they are having difficulty. Sometimes the memory of a similar real experience arouses strong emotions which prevent a rational solution to this particular scene.

Timing cannot be rigid here; sometimes children will need help every step of the way, and sometimes they can apply the Fight Fair method and gain insights almost immediately. Try this scene with as many groups as can be handled.

Discussion   Children may suggest additional scenes from their own experiences. These scenes, if they do not violate the privacy of the home, are far more meaningful than contrived situations. If a child reports "I once broke my father's fishing rod," it affords a great opportunity to play the scene as it originally took place and then replay it to show how it might have been resolved if it had happened now.

If it becomes evident that the child has no understanding of how the parent feels in losing something he values, try role-reversal and have that child play the parent.

The literature concerned with parent-child relationships offers very little to suggest how a child might handle a frightening situation where he knows his parents will be displeased. He needs help in learning how to cope with his parents' anger, punishment, and rejection, as well as with their and his own feelings of disappointment, guilt and loss of affection.

Children need to know many alternative ways of reacting to frightening situations. From their experiences within the confines of one family, they generally learn only one way to react. Through role-playing, within the classroom "family," the child can try many different approaches.

Lesson Plan 24
"SALLY ALWAYS WANTS TO EAT LUNCH ALONE."

Aims   To help children distinguish between a child who chooses aloneness, and one who resorts to loneliness from fear or shyness.

To respect children's individual choices and ways.

To accept a child who is different and not try to make him conform with the group pattern.

Introduction   "Class, our theme for today is 'Sally always wants to eat lunch alone.' Our scene takes place in the lunchroom. Sally is sitting apart from the others at lunch and is eating alone. She seems satisfied. The other children are eating and chatting in a group.

"We need five or six children. Any volunteers?"

Procedure   If there are no volunteers, the teacher chooses children, avoiding choosing a real loner to be Sally.

Sally is sitting alone, reading or just eating contentedly. Others stop by on their way to their table and ask Sally to join them. She refuses politely.

Discussion   "Why did Sally refuse to join the others?

"Did she look shy or unhappy sitting alone? Or did she seem to prefer to be alone?

"Do any of you like to be alone sometimes? What's good about it?

"How do you feel when people pressure you to join them?"

It is not only hard for children to distinguish between a shy and a healthy aloner; many adults have trouble with this. Traditionally, we tend to regard as well adjusted only those children who are popular and enjoy socializing. But some children who are "satisfied aloners" may be psychologically healthy. They are not afraid of people, but like to exercise their own choices about when to join others and when to be alone.

The psychoanalyst, Harold Greenwald, de-emphasizes the "popular pal" syndrome, and explains that a child's choice to be alone is worthy of respect.[1]

Lesson Plan 25
"RALPH JUST HANGS AROUND ALONE. HE WON'T DO ANYTHING THE REST OF US DO."

Aims   To give the shy child a boost in his self-image.

To distinguish between the pathologically shy child and the healthy loner.

To make children aware of the power they have to help an insecure classmate overcome the worthless image he has of himself.

1. Greenwald, Harold, *Decision Therapy*, New York City, N.Y., Peter Wyden, 1973

To offer ways other than crawling into a shell for coping with shyness.

To understand some of the factors underlying extreme shyness.

To indicate that criticism without honest praise can wreck personality.

Introduction   "Class, our theme for role-playing to-day is:'Ralph just hangs around alone. He won't do anything the other kids do.' Bob, suppose you play the part of Ralph."

(Note: The rule of opposites is important here. The shy child never plays a shy child as this would reinforce an already low level of self-confidence.)

"We will also need three groups of two's because we'll divide the scenes into Monday, Tuesday and Wednesday afternoons. Each day a group will meet Ralph as he is walking to school and ask him to join them for scouts, for a party or on a team.

Take your places. Action."

Procedure   This is one of the simplest sessions to stage. Ralph walks across the front of the classroom, and two role-players approach him and extend their invitations. Ralph shyly turns down every suggestion.

Children both shy and aggressive, and those in-between, will participate in this scene. No one is made to feel ill at ease. Most children are anxious to help the Ralphs.

Discussion   After the role-play, the teacher might lead off the discussion with: "We all know how frustrated we feel when someone doesn't want to join us. Maybe we didn't realize that the person was afraid to join. I remember when I ......" (Cite personal experience here.)

"Can any of you recall a time when you felt ill at ease? What do you think caused that feeling?

"Why did Ralph refuse to join the others? Did he look unhappy? Or did he seem to prefer to be alone?

"What can Ralph's classmates do that will help him change his poor self-image?

"What might have made Ralph feel so inadequate?

"How does someone who is constantly criticized feel?

"If Ralph just keeps on feeling sorry for himself, what will happen?

"What can Ralph do about it?

"Is it possible for Ralph to change, even if his family continues to find fault with him?"

Once they understand Ralph's problem, the children can help Ralph build self-esteem by letting him know that no one will push him into any situation that is painful to him. Knowing that others consider him shy is destroying Ralph, but he does not socialize because he does not trust. Perhaps he has lost faith because his experience has been with people who have let him down, or extended too much criticism, never balanced with sincere praise. The picture Ralph has of himself is not good, and was given to him by others.

Too often a sincere, well-meaning teacher reinforces shyness by praising the quiet child for being a pleasure in the classroom. "He never talks out of turn."

Here, good is equated with quiet, shy and fearful. The child so praised has to live up to the picture the teacher has drawn and he regresses further into silent solitude to avoid criticism. The shy, withdrawn youngster feels worthless and powerless in the face of criticism.

One way to help a shy child is for the teacher and children to exchange personal experiences of reactions to criticism. To realize that people who seem self-confident have been hurt and have withdrawn on occasion has a soothing and healing property. Sharing such experiences helps build trust. The psychotherapist, Sidney Jourard,[1] has done some very useful work in this area.

See Lesson Plan 52 on Strength Bombardment, (p.138). This exercise would be an excellent follow-up activity for Ralph and the whole class.

Lesson Plan 26
"I NEVER SEEM TO BE ABLE TO DO ANYTHING RIGHT."

Aims   To help children handle criticism.

To guide children to recognize that criticism is often levelled at them with the intention of helping them improve.

To develop understanding that adults who hurt the feelings of children with their criticism may not be just mean and disapproving.

1. Jourard, Sidney, M. *The Transparent Self: Self-Disclosure and Well Being*, New York, N.Y., Van Nostrand Reinhold Co., 1971.

To distinguish between criticism that is intended to be helpful (constructive), and criticism that is hurtful (destructive), and to react accordingly.

Introduction   "Class, our theme for today sounds like something a person might say if he has been criticized so often that he is ready to give up!

"Our scene takes place in the cafeteria. A group of girls are seated at a table finishing lunch. One of the girls—we'll call her Janet—takes a comb out of her purse and starts to comb her hair."

Procedure   Select as Janet a girl who is not a target of criticism. The rest of the cast may be volunteers.

Role-play the scene twice. The first time, the other students are shocked and disgusted at Janet's breach of etiquette and react with criticism.

The second time, Janet's classmates are un-dismayed by her combing her hair at the table, but the teacher walks by. He does the criticizing. Have a different cast for this scene.

If you have a child in your class who is generally a target for criticism, ask him to be the teacher. If he refuses, forget it and ask someone else.

Discussion   "Thank you, children. Playing that scene came very naturally. It was easy for you because criticizing others and being criticized yourself happens in almost every classroom and family in the world. Believe it or not, there are some primitive peoples, like the Eskimos, who never find fault with their children. That is hard for us to imagine.

"When you think about it, you realize that much that is good has come about because of criticism. If someone hadn't been critical of the old pen and bottle of ink we wouldn't have ball point pens. What else can you think of that is an improvement that came about because of dissatisfaction with what was? Bicycles? Automobiles? Houses? etc.

"If criticism of things can be good, what about criticism of people? In the scenes that were presented, did you see anything good in the criticism? Did Janet learn a good lesson from this criticism? What was it?

"Now let us ask Janet to tell us how she felt being criticized.

"Whose criticism was more hurtful, that of your classmates or of the teacher?

"If criticism hurts our feelings, can it be helpful anyway? Or is it more likely to be hurtful?

"Sometimes our hurt feelings block our ability to think clearly. What can we do about this problem of being criticized and feeling put down?"

Mrs. Florence Rogers, an outstanding educator in the field of adult-child interpersonal relationships, played these scenes with her seventh grade class and continued with other sessions about criticism. The children's own suggestions for situations were role-played. They explored ways of handling criticism. Here are their conclusions:

It is important to analyze criticism. Say to yourself, "Is this person trying to help me or hurt me?

"If the critic has hurt me, is it because he himself is tired or doesn't feel well?

"Was the criticism justified?

"Was there a better way to make the point?

"Should I sulk and go on feeling put down or shall I try to be the very best person I want to be?"

Mrs. Rogers also feels that it is as important to oppose unjust criticism as it is to accept criticism that is justified. She impresses upon children of all ages that if they feel criticism is unfair they can act upon it. "Get together in groups, appoint a spokesman, discuss the critical point quickly and quietly, end the discussion on a positive tone."

I remember trying this with Maura, a fourth grader, who role-played this problem: Every holiday when the family visited their grandmother, Maura had to spend time baby sitting in a bedroom with her two-year-old cousin who was retarded. Consequently, Maura didn't get to play with her friends who lived near her grandmother. All efforts to reason with her mother met with the criticism, "You are a selfish girl! Think of your poor cousin and her parents!" Clearly, Maura felt she was being taken advantage of and put down unjustly. The mother felt that since Maura was the recipient of many gifts from the parents of the retarded child this obligated Maura to baby sit.

Maura called on two of her friends who lived near the grandmother. They discussed the problem and then the three children approached Maura's mother, with Ellen as the spokesman. They suggested that on the next holiday Maura be allowed to play with them. Maura's mother said "no" and the two friends departed.

But Maura's mother was impressed with the seriousness of the trio, impressed with the fact that they met with her to talk about a problem, impressed with their manner of presenting the problem. She relented and agreed to Maura's request.

I remember how that class cheered after the spring vacation when Maura reported having had a good time at Grandma's house.

Some may think this is too mature an approach to expect from young children. I say—try it! Where else will children learn how to handle criticism? Most often they are powerless in a grown-up world.

One teacher suggested to the children that if they are criticized they can borrow a behavior modification idea and respond to the criticism by saying, "I appreciate your criticism; and I also like it when you tell me about some things I am doing that are right!"

Lesson Plan 27
"WE ARE GOING TO PLAN OUR OWN TOWN AND YOU WILL EACH HAVE WHATEVER JOB YOU THINK YOU'D BE GOOD AT."

Aims To improve the low self-concept of students who are slow academically but have other skills and interests.

To show appreciation for varied talents.

To provide a situation where every child can display his strong qualities.

Introduction "Class, for our next role-playing session, you will be doing some preparation in advance. You are going to be a panel of experts planning a town. You will decide what kinds of things you do best and how each of you can contribute to the new town. Our first panel will do the role-play two days from now. For this first panel, I would like to have Diane work with Sherry, Victor work with Bob, Mary work with Ann. Sometime during the next two days you will get together in your groups of two, interview one another to find out each other's strengths.

"Let us define what we mean by our strengths. When you interview each other, ask about interests, hobbies, skills. Sometimes people are not aware of the strengths they have. Everyone has some contributions he can make to the building and planning of a new town. Help each other discover what these are."

Procedure   Save this session for a time when children know each other fairly well, and their weaknesses and strengths have emerged. Low self-esteem children often respond with: "I can't do anything;" "I don't want to be on the panel;" "I'm not smart;" "Everyone will laugh at me;" or other negative responses. Encourage such children to give it a try and mention some of their positive qualities. For instance: "I notice that you are always on time;" or "I see that you like woodworking;" or "It doesn't matter if you do not have a hobby, Mary. Everybody knows that you are always ready with a helping hand."

For the first panel, pair off a high-achieving, confident child with a low-achieving, insecure one. Panel members sit around a table so that all can be heard and seen by the class. Suggest that everybody list five strengths for each child so that all will seem equal. Each member of the pair presents the strength of the other.

EXAMPLE: Sherry reports: Diane wants to be a nurse when she grows up. I think she would make a good nurse for our new town hospital because

1. She is kind.

2. She loves little children.

3. She helped take care of her little brother when he was sick.

4. Other nurses would enjoy working with her.

5. The patients would like her because she isn't crabby.

Discussion   "Does everyone have both strengths and weaknesses? How can we find these out?

"A writer once said, 'There isn't anyone in this world that we can't learn something from?' Do you agree?"

The teacher should use every opportunity to provide each child with insights into his own valuable qualities. Too often a teacher approaches helping a child from the child's weak side, instead of starting the uphill climb by giving the child a lift from his strong side.

Lesson Plan 28
"JILL'S PARENTS ARE GETTING A DIVORCE."

Aims   To lift the burden of guilt from a child whose parents are involved in divorce.

To ease the depressed and confused feelings of a child of divorce.

To give hope for a better way of life.

To help the child understand that parents are victims of their experiences, too.

Introduction   "Class, today we are going to role-play the theme 'Jill's parents are getting a divorce.' Jill is at home and hears her parents arguing. They could be arguing about the fact that Dad travels a great deal and is away from home constantly. Mother wants him to change jobs, but he refuses. They quarrel and finally decide that only a divorce will restore peace to the family. Jill is very sad and wishes she could do something to change things.

"Gerald, would you be the father; Martha, the mother; and Lois, you can be the child, Jill. You may choose a sister or brother if you wish."

Procedure   Select well-adjusted youngsters for this activity. Never call upon a child who is going through this experience even if he volunteers. This role-play is non-directive and should not pinpoint the student who is actually living through a divorce in the family.

Choosing a Mr. and Mrs. may elicit giggles, but it is less apt to cause self-consciousness than asking for volunteers. If the children refuse Mr. and Mrs. roles, the teacher or other adult can play one part.

Limit action to two to three minutes. Use a second cast if the first cast failed to project a convincing argument.

Discussion   "There we have it, class: two people who have different ideas about how they want to live. Our concern today is with Jill and how she sees herself in this problem. What do you think Jill is feeling when she hears her parents discuss divorce?

When would be a good time for her to discuss her feelings about this problem with her parents?

How can she understand the ordeal her parents are going through?

"Can Jill do anything to change things?

"How can Jill adjust to her parents' divorce?

"Sometimes divorce is a very good step. Do you know of any successful divorces?"

In the discussion, the teacher must exert every effort to protect the privacy of the home. He should guide the discussion toward impersonal ideas, rather than allowing specific examples from real life. The child of divorce in the classroom may be silent, or may plunge into the discussion. Allow his personal preference to prevail.

One teacher who tested this theme reported that her child of divorce remained quiet throughout the discussion. Weeks later, the child stopped by the teacher's desk and said he was glad he wasn't the only one whose parents were living apart. The teacher felt that he was accepting his situation more comfortably after that, and that some of the burden had been lifted.

Lesson Plan 29
"I'M MOVING TO ANOTHER STATE."

Aims   To express feelings about facing new and uncertain situations.

To build secure feelings in situations that provoke doubt, discomfort and anxiety.

To offer comfort and reassurance to someone who is worried.

To empathize with someone with a problem.

Introduction   "Today I would like one of you to pretend that your mother and dad have told you that you will soon be moving to another state. You will have to leave your school and friends behind. You have told me about this, and I have just asked you to tell the class."

Procedure   "Jane, come up on stage and tell the class. Class, when Jane is through, you can tell her how you feel about her moving. See if you can put yourself in her place. How can you try to comfort her and help her overcome her sadness? All right, Jane, you may begin."

Give Jane a few minutes to describe her plight to the class. If you feel she has not brought out her feelings, question her about them before she calls on classmates for comment. Questions might be: Jane, how do you feel about moving? What do you think you will miss? Do you know any people where you are going to move?

Discussion Transiency is a major problem plaguing educators in all grade levels.

"Class, what would you say to Jane that would help her feel better about moving?

"Have any of you ever had to leave friends behind and move away? What helped you to overcome your anxiety about breaking ties with a place and people where you lived?"

"Did you find any nice surprises in your new environment?"

"Is accepting change a necessary part of life?"

"Think about some of the people we have read about in stories, famous people in history, famous people in the news today, have any of them had to move to new places? Did they accept the change? How?"

"Can sharing our own similar experiences be helpful to Jane?"

Lesson Plan 30
"I'M AFRAID OF SPIDERS."

Aims To indicate that although fear of insects or animals may seem absurd, it is very real to the person who is afraid.

To discuss ways of desensitizing fears.

To discourage the taunting of others about their fears.

Introduction "Class, the theme for today's role-play session is 'I'm afraid of spiders.' Lots of people are afraid of insects, snakes, mice, and other animals. They may know that these things are harmless, but they are still afraid.

"In our scene, two friends are walking home from school when suddenly, from behind a bush, a boy leaps out and dangles a spider in front of them. One of the children is frightened and runs. The other one has no fear of the spider. When the boy leaves, the first child rejoins the friend and they discuss the experience. Have we any volunteers?"

Procedure   An all too well known scene, this action is easy to reproduce in the role-playing session. Props like a rubber spider, or a plastic snake, will add to the performance.

In this situation, it is recommended that shy children be encouraged to participate. There is no threat to their self-consciousness because the mood is light. If the aggressive tease is cast here, the attention and applause may reinforce his negative needs. On the other hand, the teacher may want to implement role-reversal to give the tease an opportunity to feel the impact of his teasing on others.

Action should be quick. Two or three casts are possible in one session.

Discussion   "Thank you, children. We have had a good laugh and we enjoyed watching this situation. But what about the person who has such fears? What do you think causes these fears?

"How can we try to rid ourselves of these fears? A sixth-grade teacher I know was afraid of mice and so were some of her students. They decided on a plan to see if they could overcome their fear of mice. First, they tried to find the origin of each person's fear. Some didn't know, and some traced the cause back to having been scared by a mouse.

"Next, they did some research and reported to each other all the information they could find about mice. Someone brought in a cage of mice and it was kept in the classroom for the group to take care of. Their anxiety began to dissipate, and at the end of their experiment six out of eight lost their fear of mice. The other two were less apprehensive, but announced 'We still hate mice!'

"How do you feel about people who criticize you for your fears? How can we deal with this?"

Many variations on this theme are possible. Children often express fear of the dark, of thunder, of deep water, and other natural phenomena. Although they may be powerless to control the fear, often the mere discussion is therapeutic.

Lesson Plan 31

"IF I TELL WHO TOOK THE ANSWER SHEET, I'LL GET BEATEN UP. IF I DON'T TELL, MY WHOLE CLASS WILL SUFFER."

Aims   To clarify where responsibility lies.

To clarify the difference between "squealing on someone" and taking socially responsible action.

To measure the long-range effects of honesty versus the short-term effects of dishonesty.

To discuss respect for others and respect for self.

To discuss what's involved in having the courage of one's convictions.

Introduction   "Class, listen closely to our theme for today's role-playing session: 'If I tell who took the answer sheet, I'll get beaten up. If I don't tell, my whole class will suffer.' How often have you been faced with a situation where you can't decide what to do? After the role-play we'll discuss our ideas."

Procedure   "Here is the scene: A girl or boy tiptoes into the empty classroom, glances around quickly, doesn't see anyone, rifles through the papers on the teacher's desk, finds and takes the answer sheet to the math test. Meanwhile, another student who has been in the room, kneeling by his chair, has seen what was happening. The teacher walks in unaware that anything is wrong. The student who took the answer sheet does not know that he was seen. The student who witnessed the theft has to decide what to do about it."

The action may go on for three minutes or longer. Because of the seriousness of this theme, it may be advisable to allow time for mental incubation before the discussion period. Children may want to discuss this problem with parents and friends outside the classroom.

The teacher may decide to have both the role-play and the discussion in the same session, or to postpone the discussion of this theme to later in the same day or to the next day. The students may want to replay the scene; some of them may be eager to volunteer for the role of the theft-observer.

Discussion   "Let's combine our ideas and see if we can come to some conclusion about what is the best thing to do in this case. My first question to you is: What thoughts would go through your mind if you were in this situation? What would you do?

"Is withholding the truth dishonest? What is the responsibility of the one who witnessed the theft?

"Is self-respect or liking yourself worth a beating?

"What would happen in a society where most people refuse to get involved? What would happen if most people minded only their own business?

"We can see that there are many different points of view and many alternative choices of action. Each person has to choose what is best suited for him."

Care should be taken to respect the views of all. The important thing is that the children see that there are alternative ways of behaving. It is the responsibility of the teacher to give the child greater awareness, but it is the child's decision to change if he desires to do so.

This theme provides interesting material for a role-play session for an assembly program or a PTA meeting. Role-play it in at least three ways to demonstrate different solutions and their effects:

1. Witness interrupts and confronts the wrongdoer

2. Witness tells the teacher

3. Witness does nothing

Lesson Plan 32

"ROBERT STOLE THE VOLLEY BALL FROM THE GYM AND HID IT IN HIS LOCKER."

Aims   To confront a wrongdoer.

To solve the problem of a theft in school by peer intervention strategy.

To discuss the best means for constructive action-taking where risk is involved.

To indicate to the wrongdoer what courses of action he may take if he chooses.

To give a wrongdoer a chance to observe positive ways to respond to being caught.

Introduction   "Class, our theme for today's role-play session is, 'Robert stole the volley ball from the gym and hid it in his locker.' One of you will play Robert, and one of you will take the part of the student who saw him take the ball. You will work out the scenario by yourselves. We will try it a few times with different casts."

Procedure   "Our scene takes place after one of you has seen Robert hide the ball in his locker. You confront him immediately."

This is a rather difficult problem for young children. Usually denial is the wrongdoer's weapon, followed by anger and physical threats to the confronter. Allow the children to role-play this reality.

Avoid selecting actors for the part of wrongdoer

who may fall into this role in real life situations. Class role-models give the best ideas for peer intervention strategies. The real life wrongdoer gains insight by seeing how much more fruitful it would be to handle this situation differently.

Suggestions for behavior change that are not actually directed at a wrongdoer and come from peers are far more powerful in motivating behavior change than lectures from a threatening adult authority figure who states you ought to or you shouldn't do this.

Discussion   "Thank you, children for the way in which you played your scenes.

"Now I'd like to tell you the ideas of a class in Encino, California, who role-played this scene. We can compare our acting with theirs. They listed five things that they thought were important for someone who was caught doing something wrong:

1. Don't get angry.

2. Admit it.

3. Promise you won't do it again.

4. Go on as if nothing happened.

5. Try hard not to make the same mistake again.

"They also thought these four things would be important if you caught someone in the act of wrongdoing:

1. Keep your cool.

2. Speak to the person alone.

3. Tell what you saw without name calling.

4. Don't threaten to tattle-tale.

"What do you think of these ideas?

"Why is it important for the wrongdoer to listen calmly?

"Do you agree that he should admit to the act of wrongdoing?

"Why should the wrongdoer make a promise that he won't do it again? Will it remind him if he is tempted again?

"Why should he just forget his action and go on as if nothing happened? Will it help him make a new start?

"Suppose his accuser is a tattle-tale. Is it still a good idea for the wrongdoer not to be discouraged in changing his behavior?

"Can someone else make us change our behavior or is it our own personal decision when we decide to improve? Does it come from deep inside ourselves?

Lesson Plan 33
"HEY, MARK, LOOK AT ME ON MY NEW BIKE!"

Aims   To share someone else's happiness.

To acknowledge feelings of envy.

To try to overcome the bitterness of jealousy.

To become more sensitive to the feelings of others when they may conflict with our own feelings.

Introduction   "Class, today our theme is: 'Hey, Mark, look at me on my new bike!' It is Roy's birthday and he has received a new bicycle. Roy has just about every kind of play equipment that anyone could want. He's a nice guy and everybody likes him. Roy is out riding his new bike when he passes Mark walking toward a friend's house. Mark is well-liked, too, but his parents cannot provide him with all the things Roy has. He desperately wants a bike and is envious of Roy."

"Let's have volunteers."

Procedure   Two minutes is adequate time. If there are Mark and Roy types in the class, avoid casting them in these roles.

Discussion   "How did Roy's happiness over his new bike make Mark feel?

"Should Roy have curbed his excitement?

"Does everyone feel envy at some time or other?

"How can we overcome jealousy?

"Could Roy have said or done something so that Mark could have shared his happiness?"

Sharing the personal experiences of teacher and class is a good idea. Children often harbor secret feelings of envy and may feel shame or guilt. Expressing it and knowing that others are also envious at times helps ease the burden.

Lesson Plan 34

"MISS HALE GIVES SO MUCH HOMEWORK, I NEVER HAVE TIME FOR MYSELF."

Aims   To provide children with recourse in dealing with a problem with an adult authority figure.

To help children realize their right to confront a teacher in a constructive manner.

To reduce the child's feeling of helplessness in a situation that he regards as unfair.

To give the child an understanding of the teacher's point of view with regard to homework.

Introduction   "Class, have you ever felt that one of your teachers gave too much homework, but you were unable to say or do anything about it? Today our theme for role-playing is 'Miss Hale gives so much homework, I never have time for myself'."

Procedure   "We are going to act out our theme in two scenes. For scene one we will need a teacher who will load the class with homework. You can all give your usual reactions to that, whether they be mumblings, complaints, or requests that Miss Hale lighten the load. She is not going to listen or change her mind.

"Following this scene, we'll have a discussion about how to approach Miss Hale about the problem.

"Then we will have scene two, in which a selected group will meet with Miss Hale to discuss calmly the problem of too much homework to see if they can arrive at a solution.

"Who would like to be Miss Hale? Come up here for scene one."

Stop action after the point has been made that Miss Hale will not yield to their pleas.

Discussion   "Thank you, boys and girls, and Miss Hale for a convincing performance.

"We cannot solve this problem until we know why Miss Hale thinks it is important to give so much homework. We know our own point of view, but what is hers?

'How can we get Miss Hale to compromise? Should we talk to her while we are still upset, or when we are calm?

"Is it better for one person to speak to Miss Hale, or a small group?

"How can we let Miss Hale know that we appreciate her concern and caring for us as a class? Can we apply the three Fight Fair (see p. 76) principles here?"

Following this discussion, the class selects a few members to make an appointment with Miss Hale about the homework situation, and scene two is acted out. If, in the discussion, several different solutions have been suggested, the scene may be acted out several times with different casts.

Children who are dissatisfied with a teacher, but feel powerless to deal with the problem react by grumbling, avoiding, or asking parents to intervene. Children can be taught to assume responsibility and to confront issues in the constructive manner. This results in improved relations between teacher and class.

Lesson Plan 35
"WHEN I GET MAD, I SAY MEAN THINGS AND THEN I HATE MYSELF."

Aims   To seek alternative ways to handle anger.

To relieve guilt feelings.

To probe the dynamics of wanting to retaliate with hurting words.

Introduction   "Class, our theme for today's role-playing session is 'When I get mad, I say mean things and then I hate myself.' Many of us have found ourselves in this situation. Sometimes we get angry when someone disagrees with us. Or we may get angry because someone has let us down or disappointed us. We may use language that we later regret.

"Our scene takes place on the playground. Rose and Beth are making plans for a picnic for Saturday when Elsie joins them. Elsie reminds Rose that she had promised to spend Saturday with her at her home. An argument develops, and in her anger and frustration, Elsie says some pretty mean things. Rose and Beth are indignant. They walk away together, leaving poor Elsie alone.

"Have we any volunteers?"

Procedure   Select three expressive youngsters who are not afraid to speak up. This is not for soft-spoken children.

Action time can be about two minutes, until the point is made.

No props or scenery are required.

A second or third cast action will add to this session. You will find that you have many volunteers for the role of Elsie.

Discussion   "Thank you, girls. How did Rose and Beth feel when Elsie screamed at them?

"How do you suppose Elsie felt for the rest of the day?

"Is feeling guilty the same as being angry with ourselves?

"What are the dangers of "keeping in" anger?

"How might Elsie have expressed her anger more constructively? Are there any good outlets for anger? Would talking the situation out with another person clear the air? Would going back after she cooled off and talking it over more calmly with Rose be a good idea?

Lesson Plan 36

"WHAT DO I DO WHEN MR. BLANK STARTS YELLING AT ME?"

Aims   To lessen the dread fear of adults who yell.

To understand why some adults yell.

To suggest ways of facing this problem.

To demonstrate that children are not altogether at the mercy of adults.

To diminish the child's feeling of powerlessness.

Introduction   "Class, we are all familiar with the ter-
ror we feel when an adult yells and screams at us.
Today our role-playing session will be devoted to the
theme: What do I do when Mr. Blank starts yelling at
me?

"Let's take this situation to act out: Two friends
are at the park playing in a sandbox. A little girl joins
them. Mr. Blank has brought the little girl to the park
and is responsible for her. He (Mr. Blank) is sitting on a
park bench reading while the children play. Suddenly,
the little girl is accidentally struck by a tool that the
children were using to build a sandcastle. Mr. Blank
does not listen to explanations. He yells and threatens
the children.

"Who will volunteer for these parts?"

Procedure   Children can set up this scene and improvise the action with little or no help. If action takes
less than one minute, then a second and third cast can
be chosen.

Children are generally willing volunteers for this
scene.

Discussion   "Thank you for a lively scene. And now
let's talk about Mr. Blank. Was it fair for him to yell at
the children?

"Why do you suppose he chose to shriek rather
than talk over what happened? Is there something Mr,
Blank feels guilty about or is afraid of? Do you think his
yelling has become a habit?

"What can we do so that we will not be shattered
by people who scream at us? Might the Fight Fair

Method (see p. 76) be a respectful and proficient way of facing a 'screamer'?

"Another possibility, when someone yells at you, is to try simply saying, 'I like it better when you speak softly.' Repeat this a few times. The person may become aware of his yelling and calm down. Has anyone had such an experience in real life? Perhaps you can tell us about it, or act it out."

One of the most devastating experiences that a child has to cope with is being yelled at by an adult—who is all-powerful, bigger, stronger, and angry. Most children have no recourse but to "take it." However, to continue with this blind obedience is destructive to both the "screamer" and the child. Alternative ways of reacting to adult behavior that stifles the child's personality development should be encouraged. Children can realize the power of positive solutions is in their hands if they are given the right to test these solutions.

Lesson Plan 37
"I ASKED MYSELF: SHOULD I KEEP THE WALLET?"

Aims   To dramatize the assessment of values.

To give children insight into how different role-models might face temptation. (Note: A role-model,[1] as explained by Jerome Kagan of Harvard, is some signifi-

1. Kagan, Jerome, Moss, Howard, A., *Birth to Maturity: A Study in Psychological Development*, New York, N.Y., John Wiley & Sons, 1962.

cant person that a child models himself after.

In the classroom, the role-models are those children most respected by others.)

Introduction   "Class, today we are going to conduct our role-play session somewhat differently. The theme is: 'I asked myself: Should I keep the wallet?' Imagine that you are sauntering along a lonely street when lo and behold! you find a wallet on the sidewalk! You look around you, but no one is in sight. You have to decide what to do. The exercise is to speak aloud what your •thoughts are. Since this is a monologue, it will require only one person at a time. Douglas, will you be first?"

Procedure   Place a wallet with money in it in the middle of the scene. Use at least three role-models.

Comparing their values makes for an interesting discussion period.

When the children are through, the teacher, if he chooses, can act out what he would do in this situation.

Discussion   "Let's talk about what different people choose to do in this situation. How do you feel about a person who would keep the wallet?

"How do you feel about a person who would return the wallet to the owner?

"Why would someone keep the wallet? Why would someone return the wallet?

"Is respect for one's self, or being proud of one's self, more valuable than money?

"How would you feel if you were the one who had lost the wallet?"

The attitude of many children will be "Why bother to return the money?" Presumably the class role-models will provide exposure to different values. The teacher should try to keep the discussion non-judgmental. The attitude is: let's explore many different possible courses of action and their consequences; then each of us is free to choose our own pattern.

In participating in the role-play himself, the teacher is aware that he may be exercising great influence. However, if all along the teacher has encouraged free expression of opinion, the discussion will include critical reactions to all the presentations, including the teacher's.

Lesson Plan 38
"AMY'S MOTHER IS SO NICE TO ME. I WISH I COULD SHOW HER HOW MUCH I APPRECIATE IT."

Aims   To help the child who is at loss in responding to kindness.

To demonstrate the potential joy of communication of feeling responses.

To give children practice in direct emotional expression.

Introduction   "Class, have you ever found yourself wanting to let someone know how much you like him, but you are at a loss for words or actions? Our theme today is 'Amy's mother is so nice to me. I wish I could show her how much I appreciate it.'

"Our scene takes place in Amy's home. Amy and her girlfriend are playing, when the mother walks in. She invites Amy's friend to spend a few days with Amy's family at a summer resort. She also offers to call the friend's parents and talk it over with them. Amy's friend is overwhelmed with Amy's mother's generosity. She doesn't quite know how to express her joy.

"Who would like to be in this scene?"

Procedure   This session can be left entirely in the hands of the children.

Action can be up to three minutes.

Invite other casts to respond to kindnesses from different adult figures, as well as from friends, in whatever situations they may suggest.

Discussion   "What is lost when we do not respond openly to the kindness of others?

"Sometimes we are embarrassed to say what we feel. What can we do about that? If we can't say 'You've made me happy,' can we write it? What other suggestions do you have?"

Children love telling about experiences that happened to them when someone was kind. Encourage them to act out the scenes for the class.

This situation is especially beneficial for a distressed youngster, who can enjoy playing the role of the kind person or the role of the receiver of the kindness.

Lesson Plan 39
"I DON'T WANT ANY BREAKFAST, MA, I'M LATE."

Aims   To show how hunger may affect the physical, intellectual and the psychological life of the child.

To suggest that a cranky child may be a hungry child.

To explain why we may not feel hungry even though our bodies need food.

To discuss the relative virtues of breakfast versus no breakfast.

Introduction   "Class, today we will role-play the theme: 'I don't want any breakfast, Ma, I'm late.' You will probably laugh at this topic, but behind this scene lies a serious problem.

"We will need a mother, a son whom we will name Charlie, a teacher, and a student who sits next to Charlie. The action will start with Charlie's Mom putting his breakfast on the table. Charlie dashes in, refuses breakfast, runs out and on to school.

"An hour later he is sitting in the classroom half asleep. When his classmate tries to rouse him, Charlie is very nasty. The teacher calls on Charlie and he cannot think clearly."

Procedure   Action can take up to three minutes. Divide stage space in half to provide for a kitchen and a classroom. Home set requires a breakfast table. Mother, in robe and curlers, comes in with cooking utensils that suggest a nutritious breakfast.

School set has a table or two desks where Charlie and his classmate sit.

Discussion   "Thank you all for that enjoyable performance.

"Charlie said he was not hungry. He didn't feel much like eating because he was too busy worrying about whether he'd get to school on time. Can this become a habit that Charlie is developing?

"Do people ever feel hungry when they are in a rush?

"Is it possible to be hungry without knowing it? What are some of the signals?

"Can a cranky child be a good playmate or a good student?

"Many people argue that breakfast is not necessary. What do you think?

How can we help Charlie?"

A teacher who tested this theme had the "no breakfast" students make a calendar and for one month note the school hours when they felt tired and irritable. The following month, they ate breakfast and kept the same records. All but two had increased energy and better dispositions by the end of the second month. They were duly convinced of the benefits of a good breakfast.

Lesson Plan 40

"WE WERE ON THE PLANE FOR TWO HOURS, BUT I DIDN'T HAVE THE NERVE TO SPEAK TO HER."

Aims   To propose that it is possible to approach someone we don't know and initiate a conversation.

To develop different ways of introducing oneself.

To suggest that a friendly overture may be rejected without insult intended.

Introduction   "Class, have you ever been in a situation where you wanted to start a conversation with someone you didn't know, but you were at a loss for words? Our theme is 'We were on the plane for two hours, but I didn't have the nerve to speak to her.'

"Who would like to be the stranger on the plane, and who would like to be the one who would like to talk but is shy about striking up a conversation?"

Procedure   Use four or six chairs to represent two rows of seats on an airplane. The performers are seated across from each other.

Following the initial performance and discussion, other casts should role-play their ideas and suggestions for different ways of starting conversations. Children may create different scenes—a party, a playground. The teacher may also assign related themes for the following day, e.g. greeting a new neighbor or classmate.

It might be a good idea for the class to invite

another class to observe and participate in this role-playing session. Let the visiting class be the strangers on the plane and your children can try out the introductions they had previously suggested. The children will enjoy the opportunity to see how others respond.

Discussion "Class, some of your suggestions for introducing yourself to someone you'd like to speak to are excellent. Usually, people are just as eager to speak to us as we are to speak to them. But we must remember that while some people will be delighted to talk to us, others will not. We should respect their desire for privacy and not feel offended." (See Lesson#24, p. 80.)

"Let's role-play a few of your suggestions with some friendly strangers, and some who are not so friendly."

Children often want to reach out to one another in friendliness but they fear rejection. Role-playing different possibilities gives the opportunity of trying life on for size. A mature attitude means that we are ready for either acceptance or rejection for our invitation to be friendly.

For the initial role-play presentations, the teacher can choose socially adept youngsters. If this topic is repeated in subsequent role-plays, the shy or introverted child may be chosen, or may even volunteer, having gained confidence from observing role-models.

Lesson Plan 41

"IT LOOKS LIKE SANDY'S FATHER WAS DRUNK AGAIN LAST NIGHT."

Aims   To help children face the reality of things they have no control over.

To share experiences about real life problems.

To help children understand the problems a parent faces that may drive him to become an alcoholic.

To suggest ways that children may cope with this problem.

To experience the joy of extending sympathy, understanding and help to someone with a real life problem.

Introduction   "Class, our theme for today involves a very sad situation that many children have to endure. We all find that we are in very unpleasant circumstances at times. The hero of our scene, named Sandy, has a father who is an alcoholic. Our theme is "It looks like Sandy's father was drunk again last night."

"We will start the action with two of Sandy's friends calling for him to play ball on Saturday morning. He comes to the door very depressed, and he walks a little way with the boys. He tells them he can't play, but he refuses to tell why. The boys guess why and they do not question Sandy further. Sandy goes back into his house and the two friends talk over Sandy's depressed attitude.

"I will ask Bob to be Sandy, and John and Robert to be his friends."

Procedure Choose a child who has a very stable family for the Sandy role. The other two players should be fairly perceptive youngsters who can provoke an interesting discussion.

A cast of girls may add to the discussion.

A follow-up role-play could try out with Sandy some of the ideas suggested by the class.

Discussion "Thank you, children. It is clear that Sandy's problem is making him depressed. We know he can't stop his father from drinking, but is there something he can do to ease the pain he feels?

"If this is Sandy's reality, and we agree that he cannot control this part of it, then what suggestions can we offer Sandy to make life more pleasant? Perhaps we can role-play a few suggestions."

If no child proposes an idea, teacher may start with "Let's imagine that Sandy has decided to make his father's home life as pleasant as possible. What might Sandy do? Greet his Dad cheerfully? Help set the dinner table? Answer Dad's questions in an agreeable manner?"

The implication here, as suggested by Alcoholics Anonymous, is that an attitude of amiability at home has a favorable effect on the drinker and is therapeutic for the family.

Getting the problem of the drinking parent out in the open where a child can deal with it is the important, but touchy, thing here. Children are very proud of their parents and are anxious for them to look as great as every other Mom and Dad appear to be. Children tend to hide their non-proud feelings, and only express them in destructive ways. Finding out that his isn't the only father or mother who drinks lightens the child's burden. Talking about it openly and receiving sympathy and help from others can be very beneficial.

The teacher should keep the discussion very matter of fact and nonjudgmental. If there is a real Sandy in the class, he may never offer a word, but observing the action and listening are more valuable than anyone can measure.

Lesson Plan 42

"CELIA BORROWED MY MATH BOOK. NOW I NEED IT FOR A HOMEWORK ASSIGNMENT AND SHE CAN'T FIND IT AND I'M STUCK."

Aims   To demonstrate the annoyance of borrowing.

To discuss ways to say "no" to a borrower.

To show that a lender is not helping a chronic borrower.

Introduction   "Class, today's role-playing theme concerns borrowing. I'm sure you've all known someone who is a chronic borrower. Our theme is 'Celia borrowed my math book. Now I need it for a homework assignment and she can't find it and I'm stuck.'

"One of you will be Celia and one of you will be Nancy, the person who lent her math book. The action will take place with Nancy meeting Celia and asking her to give back the book. Of course, Celia has all kinds of excuses.

"Any volunteers?"

Procedure   Don't be afraid to have a chronic borrower in this scene. When he reverses roles, the borrower will gain insight into the frustrated lender's feelings. However, the borrower must not suspect that you, the teacher, consider him anything other than an objective, willing participant for role-playing.

Discussion   "Thank you, children. I don't know whether to say 'Poor Celia' for misplacing the book or 'Poor Nancy' for being the victim of a chronic borrower.

"Now let us try role-reversal in the same scene. Celia will be Nancy, and Nancy can play Celia."

Procedure   Nancy and Celia reenact the scene playing opposite roles.

Discussion   "Tell us about the feelings you experienced in the opposite roles, girls.

"If we continue to lend things to Celia, aren't we rewarding and perpetuating her borrowing habits?

"How can we discourage the chronic borrower?

"Class, let's try this scene once more, using what we've learned from the discussion. Let's have Celia try to borrow notebook paper from someone. Who would like to do this acting?"

Procedure   Children will now use the follow-up ideas for refusing to lend to the chronic borrower.

Discussion   "Thank you, children. That was a good display of putting ideas into action"

It is valuable for the class borrower to see and hear how the whole group feels about something that he doesn't regard too seriously. No one ever borrows from him, so he has no idea of the annoyance he creates.

It is also valuable for others to know that they really are not helping a borrower. Their continual lending is reinforcing his bad habit.

Lesson Plan 43
"WALTER WILL NOT TAKE NO FOR AN ANSWER AND I WIND UP SAYING OK."

Aims   To indicate that we have a right to turn down a request sometimes.

To foster the courage to say "No".

To find ways to say "No" so that hurt will be minimized.

To remove the mantle of guilt when we have chosen not to respond to someone else's feelings.

To suggest that only a firm and consistent stand will discourage the nagger.

Introduction   "Class, our role-playing session today features the kind of person who nags us into changing our "No" to his "Yes". The theme is "Walter will not take no for an answer and I wind up saying OK."

"Walter and Norman are talking on the telephone. Norman wants to finish a woodworking project for school, but Walter wants Norman to go to the bicycle store with him. Walter reminds Norman that he went bike-shopping with *him* when *he* looked for a bike. He reminds Norman of every past favor he can think of. Walter pesters and nags until Norman says "OK". They make arrangements to meet, but Norman is plenty angry.

"Have we any volunteers?"

Procedure   Start the action with Norman's phone ringing. Action time is short, one to two minutes.

Discussion   "'Thank you, children.

"Although he agreed to go with Walter, Norman was angry about it. Why did he agree? Why was he angry?

"If what he was afraid of was hurting Walter's feelings, is there some way he could say 'No' that would make it easier for both boys?

"How would Walter feel if Norman said "No"?

"Why does Norman feel guilty if Walter feels frustrated or disappointed? Do you think that Walter usually succeeds in getting Norman to comply with his wishes?

"Would it help if Norman were consistently firm in his responses to Walter?

"Have you any other suggestions for Norman? For Walter?"

Children seem to like this theme and usually have a great deal of fun with it. They are often amazed at the discussion of dealing with their own guilt feelings, and at the suggestion that they should handle a nagger with consistency and firmness.

Lesson Plan 44

"GEE, MOM, WHY CAN'T WE HAVE ONE OF THESE PUPPIES?"

Aims   To give children insight into why parents sometimes say "No".

To develop an awareness of the responsibilities involved in having a pet.

To explore ways that children can demonstrate through their actions that their promises to be responsible are not empty.

Introduction   "Class, our role-playing theme today is "Gee, Mom, why can't we have one of these puppies?" Tommy and Matthew are on their way to the supermarket with their mother. They see a boy with a box of puppies. A sign on the box reads: 'Free puppies. Take one home.' The boys stop to look at the puppies. They plead with their mother to let them take one. They promise to take full care of the puppy. But mother has heard this idle promise before and says "No!"

Procedure   If this theme is assigned a day in advance, children can prepare props—stuffed dogs and a box with a sign. They will also have time to think over their presentation.

Allow a full three minutes for the role-play.

Discussion   "Thank you, children, for your dramatization and for the work you put into setting up the scene.

"Do you think it was fair or unfair for the boys' mother to say "No"? The boys promised to care for the dog; why wasn't that enough?

"How can they prove to their parents that they are really ready for the responsibility of having a dog for their pet?

"How do you think we can build mutual trust in our relationships with our parents?"

This is an excellent theme to use if your class would like to invite another class in to watch role-play. Encourage the guests to participate in the discussion.

Another possibility is to enact this theme at a PTA meeting and have parents take part in the session.

Lesson Plan 45
"I WON'T SIT NEXT TO EUGENE, HE SMELLS BAD."

Aims   To project into the feelings of someone who has been hurt by personal insult.

To place responsibility on the shoulders of the hurt child to analyze the insult and do something to correct it.

To find ways of telling someone something unpleasant without hurting him.

Introduction   "Class, today our role-playing theme will probably make you laugh, but it happens to be a widespread and serious problem. The theme is "I won't sit next to Eugene, he smells bad."

"We will need a teacher, a student who doesn't

want to sit next to Eugene, and someone to be Eugene. We will try improvising this scene. Any volunteers?"

Procedure   Use two chairs and desks next to each other.

If there are no volunteers for the role of Eugene, teacher will take that part.

Sometimes children will volunteer to role-play an "undesirable character" if the teacher was willing to play the role.

Give the children a chance to improvise the action. If improvisation does not make the point, suggest the following action: The teacher is assigning new seats to everyone. When she places Victor next to Eugene, he objects strongly. The teacher questions him and Victor does not hesitate to say frankly and honestly why he won't sit next to Eugene. Eugene's feelings are hurt.

Discussion   "Thank you, children. How did Eugene feel?

"What causes a bad body odor? Can Eugene do something about this problem?

"How could Victor have handled this problem more tactfully?

"Is there something we can or should do for people who have been hurt by others?

"What is Eugene's responsibility in this matter?"

Lesson Plan 46
"JEAN IS SUCH A SHOW-OFF, I JUST CAN'T STAND HER!"

Aims   To uncover the braggart's inner feelings of insecurity.

To help children understand that people are not always on the inside what they seem to be on the outside.

To gain insight into why some people feel it necessary to show off.

To explore the concept of a self-image

Introduction   "Children, our role-play session today is about someone who brags and shows off a lot. We all tend to react with irritation to braggarts, but perhaps if we understand why people become boasters, we will be more sympathetic.

"Our theme is: 'Jean is such a show-off, I just can't stand her!' Our scene takes place on the playground. A group of girls are chatting amiably about a boy they all admire when Jean joins them. Jean boasts that she knows him better than anyone else. The conversation then turns to the coming election for class officers. Jean asserts that she ought to be president.

"Who would like to be Jean? We also need a group of about three or four girls."

Procedure   This scene offers a good opportunity to select one or two of the shy children who do not volunteer to participate if they have to speak. In this situation, they do not have to say anything as long as there is one strong spokesman in the group. The fact that a shy child gets up is a good enough start. Talk will come later when he begins to feel more comfortable.

Action time can be a full three minutes.

A cast of boys operates in the same manner, with the braggart boasting about athletic prowess, popularity with girls, etc.

Discussion   "Thank you, children. It certainly is unpleasant to be around a braggart, isn't it?

"Is Jean aware that she is showing off?

"What does Jean really want from us when she brags?

"Does everyone need approval? Does everyone need to be liked by others?

"If we all have this need, why do some of us find it necessary to boast to gain approval, while others do not?

"Apparently, if we approve of ourselves, we are fairly confident that others will approve of us, and we don't have to make believe we are different or better than we really are. The opposite is also probably true. If we don't like ourselves, we feel that others won't like us, and we pretend to be better than we think we are.

"Who can explain what a self-image is?

"Where do we get this image of ourselves from? Name some people who give us our self-image.

"In Jean's case, what do you think happened to give her such a poor self-image?

"Can she help herself?

"How can we help her?

"Do you think that as her self-image improves, her bragging will diminish?"

"We are going to try an exercise in role imagery. It may help you learn something about your own self-image.

"Everybody relax, close your eyes, rest your head on the desk. Try to empty your mind of all thoughts. Relax and be comfortable.

"We are going to take an imaginary trip. Step out of your body and walk through a large, open field. It is a warm, sunny day and you feel very content as you move along. Up ahead you see a bench. You walk to the bench and sit down and rest. The real you is still sitting here in the classroom, but the imaginary you is on that bench in the field.

"Study that you sitting on the bench. Do you like what you see? What things do you like? What don't you like? Are your feelings strong, or are they uncertain? Try to become aware of your feelings. What would you like to say to yourself?

"Now it is time for the imaginary you to leave the field and walk back to the real you. You may open your eyes.

"If anyone cares to share any part of this experience with us, we'd appreciate hearing about it.

"Perhaps you can try working on one of the features you don't like about yourself, and next week we can take this imaginary trip again and see if you have made any change in your own self-image."

Personality theorists, such as Gordon Allport and William James, agree that self-concept is one of the basic determinants of all human behavior.[1] It is possi-

1. LaBenne, W. and Greene, Bert. *Educational Implications of Self-Concept Theory,* Pacific Palisades, Ca., Goodyear Pub. Co., 1969, pp.2-3.

ble for even young children to become sensitized to the workings of the self-image in themselves and others.

Lesson Plan 47
"A NICE THING HAPPENED TO ME TODAY......"

Aims   To permeate the classroom with an atmosphere of pleasant feeling.

To help the angry or hostile child change his mood.

To sensitize children to the positive facets of their daily experiences.

Introduction   "Our theme is: 'A nice thing happened to me today.' I'd like each of you to complete that thought in your mind. Then we will act out your experience. If you need one or more actors for your scene, you may select them. There are no time limits."

Procedure   Because this is somewhat different in format, and calls upon students to recreate real experiences, it is advisable for the teacher to provide examples from her own experience first. It can be the simplest joy: meeting an old friend, being invited to share in an activity, receiving a surprise letter or phone call, helping an old (blind) person cross the street, bringing a lost dog (wallet) back to his owner, receiving a compliment from someone you respect, sharing a goody. When the children see the types of experiences that enhanced the teacher's day, they will quickly search through their own experiences.

Mrs. Gottschall, a second-grade teacher in Ohio, tells of a touching experience of one of her children. This child had never been taught to say "Thank you" at home. No family member ever expressed appreciation in that phrase. When this child said "Thank you" to the grocer, he responded favorably. This was a new experience for the child, who acted out the scene in class, explaining that it had made her feel "good inside."

Discussion   This theme can be repeated often, but is most successful when used spontaneously. The best time to introduce it is when the teacher spots that a depressed or angry child has brought into the classroom carried-over hostilities from previous hours (trouble at home, a fight in the hall, etc.) If the timing is right, before his anger erupts into disruptive behavior, the child may benefit from sharing the feelings of someone else's joy. Anger dissipates dramatically in a joyful atmosphere. Depression lifts when it must move over and let joy in.

Would it be more effective to deal directly with the child's unhappiness? This may, ultimately, become necessary. But I have found that if the child can put aside his anger for awhile, his anxiety may be dissipated and his problem may be dealt with more easily in private later on.

Multi-sensory communication is a strong and durable monument to learning. If all senses—auditory, visual, kinesthetic and olfactory—are involved, how much greater the imprinting on the brain field than when learning relies primarily on reading and listening cues. Intellectual, physical and emotional forces must be integrated for optimum learning to take place.

This is one of the simplest themes, and requires very little discussion. The good mood that is captured when someone acts out a happy event, however inconsequential, communicates an effective lesson to the explosive characters in the classroom.

This technique is recommended for counselors, speech therapists and group leaders for use as a warm-up idea.

Lesson Plan 48
"A NICE THING HAPPENED TO ME THE OTHER DAY . . . . . ."

Aims   To structure a planned-in-advance role-play session.

To directly involve an angry child in a situation in which he is asked to express some of his brighter feelings.

To give "the loser" an opportunity to participate in a successful experience where he will gain approval and can build a better self-image.

Introduction   "This time we are going to plan our role-play theme in advance. I will tell you the theme and choose the actors. Then I will give you time to prepare your scenes. The theme is: 'A nice thing happened to me the other day . . . .' Ann, Robert, and George, I would like you to think about this theme so that each of you can act out a scene for us this afternoon (or tomorrow). If you need more people for your cast, you may select additional children. As for the rest of the class, I request that if you are asked to be in a scene, please cooperate and be helpful."

Procedure This theme is similar to the previous one (Lesson Plan 47, p. 128). It should be used after one (or more) sessions of the first theme have been carried out. The important focus is to get the hostile child involved. The other children chosen should be very popular children who can be relied upon to work independently. This will leave the teacher free to help the hostile child prepare his scene.

The practical arrangements—times for planning, rehearsals, performances—can be made as the teacher sees fit.

Discussion All too often, the disturbed, angry, or depressed child considers as rewarding those experiences that involve a destructive act, including attack or revenge in some form. The aim of this lesson is to try to guide the child, without verbal exegesis or criticism, to a more positive experience that was rewarding. Help him become aware of the gratification inherent in a constructive experience. It is not unusual for a distressed youngster to retain a sharp memory for all the ils that befall him and only a vague memory for happy times. "Injustice collectors" start early in life.

There is a tendency among all of us to equate good experiences with special times like birthdays, vacations, Christmas and the like. Emphasis on these large, broad, past experiences causes children to lose sight of the here and now value of simple joys. Youngsters, even the very distressed ones, have a built-in radar for picking up the feel and sound of appreciation. If we transmit to them how gratifying we find the small, kind, and pleasant exchanges that are to be found in everyday occurrences, we will alert them to these sources of pleasure in their own daily interpersonal experiences.

Lesson Plan 49
"THE NEW FAMILY ON OUR STREET IS BLACK."

Aims   To counteract some of the prejudice that exists.

To gain insight into some of the reasons why some people are prejudiced.

To open young minds and hearts to people of other races.

To assert the right of the individual to choose his own values.

To approach the issue of living in an integrated society from a positive and constructive point of view.

To provide an experience in taking positive social action despite mass pressure.

Introduction   "Class, today our role-play theme is 'The new family on our street is Black.' You have been exposed to a lot of positive and negative propaganda on this subject. Almost every day we read in the newspapers, or hear on television, about some terrible unkindness that has been leveled at someone with different beliefs or customs, or religion, or language, or style of dress, or color.

"Today we will pretend that a new family is moving in next door to you. They are Black, and you have heard some people in the community make disparaging remarks about them even before ever having met them.

"Imagine that you are a child who wants to make other people feel welcome and happy. You don't care if they are white, yellow, black, or polka-dot, as long as they are nice folks so that you can like them. So you decide to ignore what others have said and see for yourself what kind of people your new neighbors are."

Procedure "We'll start the action with the family moving some things from their car into the new house."

Call for any volunteers to be the members of the new family. Call on specific children, one by one, to come up and greet and welcome the new neighbors.

Each child could take about one minute. Allow the action to continue if the improvisation is interesting.

Be ready to do some role-reversal if there are any signs of bigotry. Have the bigots play the roles of the people they dislike.

Discussion "Thank you, children. You have given some very kind greetings.

"Why do people bother to be nice to each other? How would you like to be treated if you were one of the children in that Black family?

"Why do you suppose some people are afraid of anyone who seems different?

"Why are people afraid of change? What would the world be like without change?

"How many of you would want to make up your own minds regardless of what others say?

"How many of you would not be afraid to express or act on your opinions even if they were different from the opinions of others?"

This theme can be repeated with other groups that are looked upon as different.

Children often ask "What if they aren't nice to us?" This can be a theme for a future session.

Lesson Plan 50
"BOY, I SURE WISH I HAD SOME KIND OF A JOB."

Aims   To demonstrate the value of courteous manners in applying for a job.

To offer a simple plan, the GISIT method, as a useful tool in job hunting.

To discuss the applicability of interview manners in other situations.

Introduction   "Children, so many of you are interested in doing odd jobs to earn extra money. Our theme for today is 'Boy, I sure wish I had some kind of a job.' We are going to role-play some interview scenes with a prospective employer, who may be a stranger, or our grandmother, or a neighbor.

"There is no right way, or wrong way, so do what

is natural for you. After the scenes are played, we will discuss ways to strengthen our interview. Let's start with two volunteers. One person will be the prospective employer and one will be the job hunter."

Procedure   This requires no advance planning. Give the volunteers a few minutes to decide on their roles and set their scene. When they have finished, call on two more sets of children to present scenes.

After all the scenes are played, the teacher introduces the GISIT system. After writing the following five steps on the board, the teacher role-plays a scene demonstrating their use.

1. Greeting

2. Identify yourself (Name - address)

3. Skills

4. Intent

5. Thanks

Example   TEACHER, PLAYING JOHN: "Hello, I'm John Jones. I live at 20 Dearborn Street. I belong to the school band. We're washing cars in the neighborhood to earn money for our band instruments. We are charging 75 cents per car. May I make an appointment to wash your car?"(Teacher may use a child to play the role of prospective employer, or play both roles himself.)

PROSPECTIVE EMPLOYER   No, thank you. I just had my car washed.

JOHN   Thank you for your attention. I'd like to leave this card with you. It has my phone number on it, in case you know someone who needs a car wash. I'd appreciate your passing along the information.

PROSPECTIVE EMPLOYER   All right, I'll be glad to do that. Good-bye.

Discussion   "What differences were there between the approaches of the children who went first and my approach?

"Why is it important to greet the person who may be a prospective employer?

"Why should you identify yourself?

"Why is it important to get to your skill immediately?

"Is the purpose of your job important to the employer?

"Suppose the people you call upon are rude. Should you still be courteous? Why?"

This has been one of the most popular role-play lessons. Children of all ages, and from every socio-economic and cultural level, seem eager to enjoy the rewards of courtesy and good manners.

After the teacher has demonstrated the GISIT method, he may call upon the three original sets of volunteers to replay their scenes using this method. The class may then discuss and compare the two versions.

Lesson Plan 51
"GUESS WHO WAS SO NICE TO ME YESTERDAY."

Aims   To demonstrate the joys of both receiving and doing kindnesses for others.

To create a spirit of generosity and togetherness in the classroom.

Introduction   "Children, our theme is: 'Guess who was so nice to me yesterday.' Tomorrow, you are all going to be detectives. You will have to solve a mystery. Someone is going to do unexpected kindnesses for you, and by tomorrow afternoon, you have to guess who that person is.

"The kindness might be holding the door, or offering to share a snack, or helping someone carry something, or any of hundreds of small, nice things you can do for others. Be alert and as creative as you want. You may try to throw your detective off the track by being kind to other people as well."

Procedure   Each child writes his name on a small piece of paper and folds it. Names are placed in a box or hat and each child picks one, keeping the name secret. During the rest of the day and the following day, each child does one or more acts of kindness for the person whose name he has picked.

At the end of the second day, each child is called upon to guess who picked his name. He must identify the "suspect" and tell what was done.

Allow time for everyone in class to come up and

show what a good detective he was. For example:

"It is time now, children, for each detective to identify his suspect. Let's start with Alice. Did you solve the Kindness Mystery, Alice?"

ALICE   I suspect that Robert had my name because he offered to unchain my bike yesterday, and today he said "Hello" to me in the hall.

TEACHER   Robert, is this true?

ROBERT   Yes, I had Alice's name.

And so on.

Comment   Although this is not, strictly speaking, a role-play situation, children love this mystery game and will ask to repeat it again and again. Some classes have extended the game to include the children in other classes.

When children do kindnesses, they want to be recognized. If someone guesses the wrong person—which is possible if children are showering their kindnesses about generously—ask the correct child to identify himself, and be sure to praise his efforts.

Lesson Plan 52
"WHAT I LIKE ABOUT BENNY IS . . . ."

Aims   To give an immediate reward to someone.

To strengthen a poor self-image.

To impress upon children the power of praise.

Introduction   "Boys and girls, today we are going to try a new kind of bombing. It is called 'Strength Bombardment'.

"Our theme is: 'What I Like About Benny Is. . . .' Now I will ask each person in the class to state something nice about Benny."

Procedure   "I will be first. Benny, I like the way you accept your job when you are a monitor.

"You take it from there, John." John may say Benny plays fair. The next child may say that Benny is always pleasant. Another child may say he never pushes in line, etc., until all have spoken.

Discussion   "Very good, class. The next time we do this, you may select the person for strength bombardment.

"Benny, did you know the wonderful things we all think about you? How did it make you feel to hear all this?

"Sometimes we feel very low and it's nice to be reminded of our good points. Is there ever anyone who doesn't have some good points?"

Although this is not, strictly speaking, a role-playing situation as such, it may be used as a follow-up for any session. I call it a Strength Bombardment Session.

Children beyond fourth-grade level tend to become embarrassed by openly giving and receiving on the spot compliments. One of the qualities we need to develop early in life is ease in expressing admiration and affection for others. When a child grows up sensitive to the goodness of others and can communicate it, he becomes a loving adult.

This theme is especially useful when initiated spontaneously whenever a child needs a boost in self-concept. For example, suppose a child in your classroom is the victim of some unhappy incident or circumstance. Instead of referring directly to the incident, try bombarding the child with praise elicited from his peers. For example, Benny finds out that he has to wear very thick glasses. He comes to school very dejected. This is a perfect opportunity for a strength bombardment session. Of course, since this is not role-play, but direct involvement, the teacher needs to use tact and judgment.

There will be times when it will be hard for a child who doesn't really like Benny to find something nice to say. If a child ponders too long, let him pass and come back to him later. Sometimes the teacher can help this child by asking if he agrees with something someone else has said about Benny.

At a later time, Benny may be feeling better about himself and may be approached more directly about his feelings about having to wear thick glasses.

Also, Lesson Plan 47 (see p. 128) may be used to encourage Benny to look at the brighter side of life.

6

The Use of Role-Play in Subject Areas

The recent trend toward integration of subject matter wisely throws the focus on the development of the whole child, rather than on his math or science or reading or writing skills. It is recognized that creative activities promote and involve all these skills simultaneously.

The lesson plans contained in this chapter would seem to be more heavily weighted in their relevance to specific subject areas. However, it will readily be seen that these lessons also involve skills in all areas. Although physically separated from the previous lesson plans in this book, it is not intended that they be used separately, or after the others, any more than it is intended that the others be used sequentially. We leave it to the teacher to decide which lesson he will use at any particular time and to set up his own sequence.

These themes should serve as a springboard for teacher and class creativity. Art projects, costume design, scenery building, compositions, poetry and other delightful learning experiences will evolve during the use of these themes.

MATHEMATICS

One of the most effective uses of role-playing is to bring to life the problem situations that children meet in math books. It is especially helpful to a child who cannot visualize the text. Seeing the problem become a living situation clarifies it and brings the solution to light.

The following are some samples from an arithmetic book.

Lesson Plan 1
THE CANDY STORE

Mrs. Jones went to the ice cream store to buy three ice cream pops for 10¢ each. How much money did she have to pay?

Procedure   "Children, I would like all of you to read Problem 6 and imagine that we are in the ice cream store. Let's role-play this scene. Bill, would you like to be the storekeeper? We'll call him Mr. Arkin. Joan, would you like to be Mrs. Jones?"

Children come up to the stage area. Props may be used.

Teacher chooses children who are good in math so that poor math students may observe first. For subsequent problems, teacher may call on the students with math-phobia, or may simply ask for volunteers. It will be interesting to see if they volunteer on their own. Here are two scenes that took place in one classroom

Scene I

MR. ARKIN   Good morning, Mrs. Jones. What can I help you with today?

MRS. JONES   Good morning, Mr. Arkin. I want to buy three ice cream pops. How much are they?

MR. ARKIN   They are 10¢ a piece. Here you are.

MRS. JONES   How much do I owe you? (Class is called upon to volunteer answers. Real or play money is used to complete the transaction.)

Scene II: Another customer enters store.

MR. BROWN   Do you sell candy?

MR. ARKIN   Yes, I do.

MR. BROWN   Okay. I want a large bag of M&M's. How much?

MR. ARKIN   That's 50¢.

MR. BROWN   Fine. Here is $1.00. (The class is called upon to say how much money Mr. Brown should get back.)

MR. ARKIN   Here's your bag of M&M's and your change.

With a little planning, children can bring in real objects, real or play money, and set up their own store. They may plan the action and then present their role-play scenes before the class. The problems may come right out of the math textbook, or they may be invented by the teacher or by the children themselves.

THE GIFT AND THRIFT SHOP

Math lessons can really come to life if the children have a long-range goal. All the processes leading up to that goal take on a reality that motivates excited and absorbed involvement.

The lesson ideas that follow have the goal of raising money for a worthwhile cause. The project is the setting up of a Gift and Thrift Shop in the classroom. The work will sometimes involve the class as a whole, sometimes small groups of children and sometimes individual children.

If possible, it's extremely rewarding to have a *real* Gift and Thrift Shop. The toys and supplies can be donated by the children, by the children's friends, neighbors, relatives, from their own overstock or discards. Some supplies (e.g. paper place mats, greeting cards, peanut brittle, cookies) can be made by the children, thereby providing further learning experiences in related curricular areas (e.g. reading to follow directions.)

Or, money can be borrowed (from the teacher or the school's petty cash fund) with which to buy some items. This will provide further math practice, as items are price tagged, sold and money is paid back and profit (or loss) calculated. At the same time, children will be learning (in subsequent lesson plans) about actual business procedures.

Of course, if this is not possible, you can still run a pretend Gift and Thrift Shop, using any items in the classroom, or pictures from magazines.

The scenes that follow require advance planning. The suggested lesson plans can be used separately without losing their lifelike quality.

Some of the children may volunteer to be book-keepers and statisticians to keep financial reports. They catalogue the inventory and record cost. They record sales and expenses and determine profit. They can show by bar and circle graphs how the shop is progressing.

Possibilities for incorporating creative writing, English, art, social studies are endless.

Lesson Plan 2
WHERE DO PEOPLE GET THE MONEY TO SET UP A STORE?

Aims   To stress the importance of accuracy in arithmetic.

To familiarize children with the workings of a bank.

To acquaint children with the money problems involved in opening a shop.

To make learning enjoyable by simulating a real situation.

Preparation   Arrange for a trip to a bank, requesting a tour and the opportunity for the class to ask any questions they have about business loans, interest, etc. Inform the bank manager that your children will be pretending to be corporation officials interested in banking information for opening a Gift and Thrift Shop.

Procedure   After the tour, all are seated comfortably.

The teacher introduces the "corporation heads," who explain that the class is planning to open a shop. They question the banker:

How much money do we need to start?

How much interest would we have to pay on a loan?

How shall we charge for items?

How do we know if the venture is making a profit?

What does the bookkeeper do?

Shall we bring our earnings to the bank for safekeeping?

Discussion Although the teacher does his best to guide the children to ask questions having to do with the lesson aims, the bankers are often so delighted to have young visitors that the topics for discussion are not limited. However, it is the job of the "corporation executives" to gather the information they will need.

Integrate this lesson with art, English composition, social studies. For example, making a map of the community showing the route from school to bank; writing briefly on "Why I Want to Be a Banker" or "Why I Don't Want to Be a Banker," or "What Impressed Me Most Was. . . ." The rewards of this kind of school-community interaction can be extended further if the children are willing to share their writing with their host at the bank, who will undoubtedly be delighted to receive their compositions.

After the trip, the class can work out problems related to the situation. For example:

If we borrow $50 from the bank at 12% interest, how much will we have to pay back?

If we make a profit of $120 and deposit it in the bank where we will get 6% interest, how much money will we have after a year?

Lesson Plan 3
HOW DO YOU CHOOSE A LOCATION FOR A SHOP?

Aims   To learn how a location for a business is decided upon.

To acquire a concept of what rent means.

To read map distances, transportation schedules.

Preparation   Plan a visit to a realtor's office. Inform him of your aims and that the class will question him. They will role-play being potential shop owners in a cooperative venture.

Provide each child with his own map of the community, a ruler, and transportation schedules.

Realtors usually have large visible maps for pinpointing areas.

The teacher may have to preteach the vocabulary of the trip to the children (e.g. real estate agent, rent).

Procedure   This lesson involves three direct activities:

1. A visit to a realtor.

2. Map reading.

3. Interpreting transportation schedules.

Discussion   The visit to the realtor will introduce the children to some of the factors involved in choosing a good location for a business venture. Many questions will be raised:

How will people get to our shop?

What would happen if we are too far from bus, train, or subway stops?

What about parking facilities?

How much rent would we have to pay if our shop is in our school neighborhood? If it is downtown?

To figure out how far and how long people might have to travel to get to the shop, have children mark the desired location on their maps and then plot the route from their homes to the shop. They might also figure out how some of their friends and relatives would get to the shop from wherever they may live. They might compare the shortest, most direct route with the actual route of whatever public transportation is available. They can compute the distance, time, and cost.

Lesson Plan 4

HOW MUCH SPACE WILL WE NEED?

Aims   To apply mathematical concepts in a practical situation.

To use blueprints.

To calculate dimensions.

To measure areas.

To plan to use space esthetically and economically.

Preparation   Invite an architect or carpenter to come to the classroom and talk to the children. The guests can explain the importance of using space efficiently and show the children blueprints.

Procedure   Designate a section of the room to be used for selling space. Have children measure this space.

Designate square and rectangular tables to be used as selling counters. Have children measure these.

Divide children into groups and have them role-play architects and plan different arrangements of the tables in the selling area.

Discussion   Some children may be able to use graph paper and make scale drawings to show where they would place the tables. Other children may actually need to physically move the tables about the room.

Compare the various plans and ask the children which they would choose for their store.

If interest is sustained, have the children measure and arrange the various items to be sold on the tables. They may try different groupings—by category, size, price.

Lesson Plan 5
SHALL WE TAKE MAIL ORDERS?

Aims   To compute the cost of mail charges.

To learn how weight, distance, and time (air service versus regular) affect mail rates.

To decide whether it would be feasible to accept mail orders.

Preparation   Ask the local post office to send a representative to the classroom. Explain that the purpose of the lesson is to decide if it would be feasible to mail out items from our classroom gift shop.

Select a few children to role-play postal assistants. You may choose children who have trouble with math. This is a chance for poor achievers to have some feeling of success and importance during a math lesson, in which they usually fail. They can greet the representative and introduce him. They will work with enthusiasm and zest to compute the cost of mail charges.

The children can bring some gift items to school to be weighed on the postal scale. Some children may bring weight watcher scales, which are small and weigh ounces.

Procedure   The postal representative will probably explain how rates are computed according to weight and distance. The postal assistants can pick out an item and weigh it. Pretend a friend in Nebraska ordered it. Compute the cost of shipping the item. Shall the customer be charged for the shipping expense? If we pay the shipping cost, can we make a profit? If we don't absorb the shipping cost ourselves, will we lose too many sales?

Lesson Plan 6
WE'RE HAVING A CANDY SALE.

Aims   To provide an experience where rounding off and division are used.

To demonstrate that math concepts are practical and meaningful.

Preparation   Children can bring in, or the teacher may provide, different kinds of small countable candies, like jelly beans, chocolate kisses, M&M's.

You will also need small bags.

Procedure   Children can work in small groups or individually for this lesson.

"Children, we are going to package your candy for sale. Before we make the packages, count how many pieces of candy you have.

"Write down how much your candy cost. Round off the cost to the nearest 10 number. For example, you will round off 59¢ to 60¢, etc.

"Our purpose is to make packages that cost us about 5¢ each or less. You must decide how many candies to put into each package. Here's how to do it. After you have counted all your candies, divide the number of candies into your rounded out cost. This will tell you how much each piece is worth. Then you can make a 5¢ package, or a 4¢ package, or a 3¢ package. If your number of candies does not divide easily into your cost, you can leave out some candies.

"For example, John Paid 39¢ for his M&M's. We'll

round that to 40¢. He received 97 M&M's. How will we divide them? It will be hard to divide 97 into 40, so let's leave out 17 of the M&M's. Now we have 80 candies. If we divide 80 candies into 40¢, we can see that each piece of candy costs ½¢, or, to put it another way, 2 candies cost 1¢. Now, how many candies can we put into a 5¢ bag? That's right—10.

"Now, suppose we want to make a profit on our candy sale. How much profit would we make if we sold a bag of 8 M&M's for 5¢? That's right—we would make 1¢ profit on each bag."

Discussion   If children work in groups with one good mathematician in each group, the process is easier and more enjoyable.

Tables can be set up and children can actually sell their packages of candy. They will then be able to compute their profit by comparing their income with their expense.

Motivation is high and teacher can follow up with hypothetical problems using the same procedure.

This activity can become complicated and frustrating. The teacher should remind the children that it doesn't matter if their work is not exact or if they don't make a profit.

Lesson Plan 7
WE'RE GOING TO EAT SOME FRACTIONS.

Aims   To motivate an interest in fractions in a delicious manner!

To dramatize a situation where fractions are necessary.

To bring reality to the math lesson.

Preparation   Plan to have three large round cakes or pies. (Loose syrupy pies are difficult to handle.) If at all possible, make the cakes with the children, using ready-mix. There's much math involved in following recipes.

You will need a pie cutter, paper napkins, paper plates.

Procedure   Teacher draws three circles on the board and sets the real cakes or pies on the table.

Ask one child to come up and cut one pie in half. As the child is doing this, the teacher sections one of the board circles in half, and labels each part 1/2.

Repeat with the second pie, having children label the two halves of the board circle.

Then section the first board pie in quarters. Erase the 1/2 labels, and re-label each piece 1/4. Children then cut one real pie into quarters. Repeat with the second board and real pie, sectioning them in quarters and labeling each quarter 1/4. Leave the third pie intact to demonstrate the concept of whole.

Then remove 1/4 from one of the pies. Ask the children how many quarters are left. Yes, 3. We can write this as $4/4 - 1/4 = 3/4$.

If we remove another piece of pie, then how many quarters are left? Yes, 2. We can write this as: $4/4 - 2/4 = 2/4$. The children should be able to see that 2/4 of the pie is the same as 1/2. Write: $2/4 = 1/2$. Then rewrite: $4/4 - 2/4 = 2/4$ as: $4/4 - 1/2 = 1/2$.

After this, the pie may be further subdivided into eighths, and the appropriate equivalencies may be shown and written ($2/8 = 1/4$; $4/8 = 2/4 = 1/2$).

The second pie, which is still in quarters, is used to repeat the demonstration and to reinforce the concrete learning.

Moving into the abstract, teacher holds up the third pie, which is whole. Ask the children to visualize the pie cut in half, then in quarters, and finally in eighths.

Imagine this pie in eighths, how many parts will there be? If I were to remove one part, how many would be left? Could someone write that on the board?

Continue with imaginary visualization of the fractions, posing simple problems.

To end the lesson, call each child to the front of the room to receive a piece of pie. Each child must identify the fraction he receives, and tell what is left.

"I have 1/8 of the pie and 7/8 are left."

"I have 1/8 of the pie and 6/8 are left," etc.

Discussion   A follow-up lesson may use a large square or rectangular cake that can be divided into sixteenths. Using a different shape is important to demonstrate that any whole shape can be divided into fractional parts.

Lesson Plan 8
WE'RE HAVING A CLOSING DAY PARTY.

Aims   To plan a party in a systematic and organized manner.

To solidify math concepts through practical application in a highly motivated activity.

Introduction   "We will have a party to mark the closing of our Gift Shop. We will use some of our profits for our party. We will have to plan our party carefully and systematically.

"What shall we have for refreshments?" (Presumably, the children will suggest candy, cake, soda.)

"We have 36 children in our class. If each person has four pieces of candy, how many will we need all together? How many pieces come in one package? How many packages will we need? If a package costs about 50¢, how much will we spend?

"If one large bottle of soda will serve six children, about how many bottles will we need? At about 65¢ per bottle, what will be the cost?

"How many dozens of cupcakes will we need? If a dozen costs 79¢, how much will the total cost be? If we want to spend less, we can divide the cupcakes in half. How many will we need? How much will we save?

"What else do we need for our party? Paper napkins, paper cups and paper plates. If the napkins cost 79¢ for a package of 40, about how much is each napkin?

"If there are 20 paper cups in a package, how many packages will we need?

"If one package costs 95¢, how much will we spend?

"A dozen paper plates cost 40¢. How many dozens do we need? How much will it cost?

"Would you like to buy prizes for the games? Or should we use some of our leftover merchandise for game prizes?"

Procedure If possible, the class should make an exploratory trip to the local supermarket to price the various items (candy, cupcakes, soda, paper goods).

They can then make a chart to show what they need, how many of each, and the cost of each. Then they can compute the total cost. If there is not enough money from the Gift Shop sales, perhaps volunteers may donate some of the items.

Lesson Plan 9
MAY I INTERVIEW YOU FOR OUR MATH CLASS?

Aims To use the community as a primary source for children's learning.

To demonstrate that math plays an important part in our day-to-day lives.

Preparation The teacher should enlist the cooperation of local service and professional people. After the teacher has paved the way, children can write for appointments to interview community people. They can try questioning gas station attendants, toy shop owners, doctors.

Procedure "Children, we are going to role-play the news reporter who interviews people. Who can describe what an interviewer does? Why is this an important job?

"We will pretend we are reporters. First we must have a reason for interviewing people. Our reason will be that we want to find out how they use math in their jobs. Here are the instructions you will follow:"

1. Ask the person for an appointment to interview him for about 15 minutes. State your purpose.

2. Be prepared. Have your questions ready. All of you will ask: "How do you use mathematics in your business life?" You may ask any other questions you think of that are related to what the person tells you.

3. Be sure to arrive on time.

4. You may want to make a few notes while you are there. Be prepared with pen and paper.

5. Be polite.

6. Be prepared to share your report with the class. You may use your notes, or prepare a written report.

Discussion   Spend some time discussing appropriate questions. A precocious fourth grader interviewed a school supervisor. One of his questions to the supervisor was "Do you cheat on your income tax?"

The class may practice interviewing you or other teachers or school personnel before they tackle community members.

LANGUAGE ARTS

Lesson Plan 1
A GUIDED FANTASY

Aims   To release creative forces in the subconscious.

To suggest that everyone can be creative since creativity flows from the collection of experiences and emotions that we bank in our memory.

Procedure   The elementary school child is not too young to understand creativity and the unconscious components of the human mind. Children are as excited to learn about their own psyches as they are to know about their own bodies.

Plan to have this session after a very active period; it relaxes. Cut out all noise and distractions, put a DO NOT DISTURB sign up.

Keep your voice low and calm.

Pause for 15 seconds between each direction during the guided fantasy.

"Class, today, I am going to take you on a guided tour of your unconscious mind. This is the part of our minds that houses our memories and feelings. When we are creative, we use these memories and feelings that we have stored in the unconscious.

"For instance, when you were very young, you may have enjoyed finger-painting. Your unconscious remembers good feelings with finger painting. Perhaps, at another time, you loved cutting out paper forms. Your unconscious stored these good feelings away, too. Then one day you wanted to try something new and different. You thought and thought, and suddenly, in a flash, your unconscious told you to try putting together finger paints and cut-outs. You did; it was a success and everyone said "How creative! Where did you get the idea?" You may have said, 'Oh, I just thought of it.' Actually your unconscious was very busy being creative.

"Today, we will allow our subconscious full reign. Our fantasy tour will have a surprise ending that we will share later, if you wish.

"Close your eyes and become as comfortable as possible. Try to relax.

"Empty your mind; don't think of anything.

"Allow whatever images come to you to drift across your mind.

"You are sitting in a field. It is a warm sunny day. You are enjoying the view around you.

"Far in the distance you see a mound that looks like a cave. You decide to explore.

"You get up and slowly walk down to it.

"You find it is a cave.

"You decide to go in.

"Inside, you look around.

"In one corner there is an old chest.

"You walk over to it.

"You pick up the lid.

"The chest is filled with jewels. You take them out.

"When you reach the bottom of the chest, you find there is something there that you have always wanted.

"Look at it for a while.

"Now quietly open your eyes. The tour is over."

Discussion   At this point, the class may share what they saw and how they felt.

"Lee, you saw a sailboat at the bottom of your treasure chest. Are there any events in your life that would suggest that your heart's desire is a sailboat?

"Were any of you surprised at your treasure? Can you connect it with any experiences that your subconscious may have hidden?"

The children may want to try this with their parents and friends. Caution them that it may not always work. Some people have more trouble relaxing than others.

There are people who are so controlled that they are programmed only to what their conscious mind can do. They find it difficult to free themselves for the joy of creative imagery.

Sometimes, it may not work the first time but may bring a better response the second or third try.

A friend of mine, Sandra Snell, works with boys who are in a home for juvenile offenders and has used this exercise with them with remarkable results. They enjoy it immensely and seem to become completely relaxed. Now they make up their own fantasy situations and use them whenever things get tense.

Lesson Plan 2
WORDS OF WISDOM CHARADES

Aims To dramatize famous quotations.

To analyze the quotes critically.

To convert abstract language into reality.

To generate philosophical statements from personal experiences.

Procedure Have children bring in a famous quotation they are familiar with and feel they have been influenced by.

Children are constantly being exposed to tons of philosophy through the sayings, homilies, proverbs, and superstitions with which adults sprinkle their speech. Some of these casually expressed viewpoints may represent profound truths. But some are thoughtless, shallow or even malicious. For example: "You must eat everything on your plate. People in Europe are starving," or "You made your bed. Now you must lie in it." These well-intentioned outrages have a tremendous impact on the bodies and minds of children..

Write the following quotations on the board, or duplicate and hand out copies. Have children contribute to this listing the quotations they have brought in.

1. The secret of happiness is having something to do.

2. No one is ever beaten unless he gives up the fight.

3. A person wrapped up in himself becomes a small package.

4. Childhood shows the man, as morning shows the day.

John Milton

5. Prejudice is the child of ignorance.

Hazlett

6. All that we send into the lives of others, comes back into our own.

Edwin Markham

7. 10% inspiration + 90% perspiration = 100% success.

8. Childhood is spent in seeking the truth; adulthood in preserving it.

9. A rolling stone gathers no moss.

Children work in pairs or in small groups acting out a quote they have selected from the listing. Class guesses which it is.

Upper grades can try their hand at paraphrasing the quotations. Example: "A rolling stone gathers no moss" becomes "A moving boulder accumulates no turf."

Children can be ingenious about acting out both the literal and figurative meanings of quotations that appeal to them. For example, one group of three children selected the fourth quotation. Each child pretended to grow from childhood into adulthood by gradually rising from a crawl to an upright position, all the while preserving the same character trait. One child was a cranky baby and grew into a cranky adult; the second grew from a happy smiling infant into a happy adult; the third was a sickly baby and became a hypochondriacal adult full of aches and pains.

To dramatize the fifth quotation, a group of youngsters donned caps and gowns and pretended that three of them were graduating. One, a black student, was given an award for top academic honors. In their next scene, the three graduates were seen applying for a job. The two white students got the job, but the black honors student was turned down.

Guide the discussion following the dramatizations toward a critical examination of the extent to which these pearls of wisdom embody eternal truths. For example, "Do they apply to our world today?" In the case of "A rolling stone, etc." consider the parents who are transferred to other cities for job advancement. Certainly, this is not an appropriate quotation for everybody today.

Children should learn to be cautious of sweeping generalizations. Raise the question "In what situations would this quotation be correct? Incorrect?"

Encourage children to try to develop their own words of wisdom by reversing the procedure followed in this plan. That is, have children write out short paragraphs briefly describing an experience they have had. (e.g. I was babysitting for my kid sister and she fell down and hurt herself and my parents were furious with me. Or, sometimes when I try too hard everything goes wrong, and when I don't really care, it comes out all right.) Form small groups and have each group choose one of these paragraphs at random. After they dramatize it, have the class try to formulate an apt philosophical quotation.

Lesson Plan 3
PLAY-READING

Aims   To deepen levels of comprehension in reading.

To gain insight into character by pretending to be a person in a book.

In a recent survey, children who were below-grade-level readers indicated an overwhelmingly positive response to play-reading. Acting out as the child reads results in a three-dimensional effect:

1. Motor - His physical being translates thoughts into motion.

2. Psychological - Interacting and reading with others, he acquires awareness, understanding and insight into character that he might have missed if he were reading in isolation. The story takes on reality and unity.

3. Intellectual - The child is forced into concentrating on the vocabulary, the sequence and meaning of the text.

For the average and the gifted student, play-reading presents a chance to expand his talents and adds diversity to his reading program.

Procedure   Here's an idea that has motivated both slow and gifted groups of children from third through sixth grades.

The class reads a biography or autobiography. The children bring in costumes, or parts of costumes that they feel go with that person.

If possible, take the class to the auditorium in costume. Half the class is then seated in a semi-circle on stage. The remainder of the group is audience. Appoint a Master of Ceremonies who will introduce each child by given name and by name of role portrayed. They do not attempt to reconstruct the whole story, but rather choose a small vignette. Allot a few minutes for presentation, and thank the presenters.

When the first group has finished, they change places with the audience. The teacher remains in the audience allowing the class independence to run their own show. Guidance may be needed for timing or speaking so that all may hear.

When the class gets pretty good at improvisational presentations, they may want to invite another class into the auditorium to see the show.

Discussion   Older children can gain deeper insights into the characters in biography, history, and literature by interpreting personality in dramatic form. They are most successful if they structure their character into a monologue or two-person sketch. The self-consciousness felt by seventh- or eighth-graders is more apt to be overcome if they are given ample time to plan.

Another useful device is to stop the reading of a book or story at a crucial point in the plot and have children dramatize what they think will happen.

Open-end stories provide creative opportunities. With younger children, the teacher reads a story to the class and withholds the ending. He asks, "How do you think this story ends?" The class is divided into small groups and each group meets in a corner to decide on their action. They take turns presenting their different versions. After all the dramatic presentations are over, the class discusses them. Then they finish reading the story and compare their endings with the one in the book.

It is possible to use the same approach after silent story reading. In this case, the motivating question may be "Can you think of another way this story might end?"

Lesson Plan 4

"THERE'S A GORILLA UNDER MY BED!"—AN INSTANT PLAY FOR READING, DISCUSSION AND COMPOSITION

Aims   To read a play in one class period and discuss the central ideas of the play: experiencing insecurity in new situations; observing that different people accept change differently; exploring ways of helping a shy and fearful child; learning that nightmares are connected with real experiences.

To give the child who fears improvisational role-playing an opportunity to gain confidence.

To integrate play reading with play writing.

Procedure   "Children, today we are going to do a show. Our play is called, 'There's a Gorilla Under My Bed!' The cast consists of five people: Jean, the youngest child; Ruth, the middle child; Bob, the oldest child; Mrs. Johnson, their mother, and a narrator.

"The action will take about seven minutes. Can I

have some volunteers for the parts? The rest of you will all be called upon to take a more active role."

The children who have volunteered are given an opportunity to read the script, gather their props,and set their scene. Meanwhile, the teacher asks the rest of the class whether they have ever had to move from one state to another. They discuss this until the actors are ready to perform.

THE PLAY: *"There's a gorilla under my bed!"*

ACT I   Kitchen of Johnson family's new home. Dinner time.

NARRATOR   Welcome, boys and girls, to our dramatic play-reading time.Today we offer you our performance of "There's a Gorilla Under My Bed!" It is a comedy and we hope you will laugh, but it is also a play with a problem we must all face: the fear of having to move into a new situation.

You will meet Mrs. Johnson, the mother of the family; Bob, the oldest child; Ruth, the middle daughter; and Jean, the youngest. The family has just moved from their home in New Jersey to Ohio. Dad is away on a business trip and Mother and the girls are in the kitchen finishing unpacking. They are all very tired. Let's listen in and see what is happening.

RUTH   Where shall I put these cups, Mother?

MOTHER   Well, we're too crowded in the cabinets already. Oh, just leave them in the carton and Daddy can put them on the garage shelf until I want to use them. *(Ruth puts dishes back and turns to Jean.)*

RUTH   Jean, why are you standing there looking so glum? Get busy! *(Jean does not respond.)*

MOTHER   Jeanie, will you help me to clear and set the table now? If you keep busy enough you won't have time to be sad. Bob should be back from the delicatessen any minute with some sandwiches for us.

RUTH   Let's make our first supper in our new home like a picnic, Mother.

MOTHER   That's a good idea. *(To Jeanie)* What do you say, Jeanie—shall we make this meal a picnic and have fun?

JEANIE   *(Very angry)* Count me out! I don't like it here. Who could have fun in this horrible place!?!

RUTH   *(Annoyed)* Listen here, sourpuss, I've been trying to cheer you up all day and now I'm getting sick of your attitude!

JEANIE   *(Angry)* Who asked you to appoint yourself my keeper?!? You're not so great, you goon! *(Ruth and Jean start toward each other to fight.)*

MOTHER   Girls! Girls! Let's cut out this bickering. We are all very tired and our tempers are short. Jeanie—find a towel and washcloth and get washed for dinner. And it's going to be a picnic dinner! *(Jeanie grumbles and exits.)*

RUTH   *(Still annoyed)* I don't know how you can stand that kid, Mother. She needs a good spanking.

MOTHER   No she doesn't, Ruth. She is feeling very lonesome right now for the friends she left behind and the worst part of this move for Jeanie is her fear that she might not make new friends. *(Ruth and Mother set table.)*

RUTH   So what? I don't like leaving my friends either, but I'm not going to make a "big deal" over it like she is.

MOTHER   Everyone is different, Ruth. Some can adjust to change better than others. Jeanie isn't finding it easy to give up the place where she felt safe and secure. Besides, she's not as confident meeting new people as you are.

RUTH   There you go, Mother, making excuses for her again. *(Enter Bob with groceries.)*

BOB   We eat, folks, we eat!! *(Sets food bag on table)*

RUTH   Sure smells good.

BOB   Here's your change, Mom. I got roast beef sandwiches and cupcakes. The delicatessen is about four blocks from here. Real cool guy owns it. I told him we were new here and he said if there's anything we want to know about the neighborhood he'd be glad to tell us. He knows everybody, I guess.

MOTHER   That's nice to hear. I'll have lots of questions for him. Did you get paper napkins?

BOB   Yes, they're at the bottom of the bag. *(Sees Jeanie)* Well if it isn't old happy face herself! How are ya' doin', Jeanie? *(No response from Jeanie. Bob smiles, shakes his head.)*

JEANIE   *(Ignores Bob)* I'm not hungry, Mother. Could I go to my room and put my books in the case?

MOTHER   Go ahead, dear. I'll be in to help you in a little while.

BOB Can I eat her sandwich?

MOTHER Honestly, Bob, sometimes I don't understand how you and Ruthie can completely ignore the feelings of your little sister.

BOB What did I do?

MOTHER Just don't tease her now while she's so down in the dumps.

BOB She's acting like a baby.

RUTH I agree with that.

MOTHER Well, let's just try to be patient with her. *(Family sets up chairs to sleep on.)*

NARRATOR The family finished their dinner and continued to unpack. Around nine o'clock they were all very tired and decided to go to bed early. They were all sound asleep when suddenly, around midnight, they were awakened by a scream.

ACT II Bedroom

JEANIE *(Screams)* Ruth, Mother come quick! *(Looks under bed, screams again)*

RUTH *(Sleepy)* What's the matter, Jeanie?

JEANIE Can I come into your bed, Ruth?

RUTH Why?

JEANIE There's a gorilla under my bed!

RUTH Oh, come on. Go back to sleep. *(Mother enters.)*

MOTHER What's all the excitement here?

JEANIE   *(Very excited)* Mother, I saw a gorilla and Ruthie doesn't believe me.

MOTHER   Calm down, Jeanie. What happened?

JEANIE   I was asleep and I heard all this noise—like something growling and I looked and there was a gorilla under my bed! He might still be there.

MOTHER   I'll take a look. *(Looks under and around bed)* No signs of any gorilla in here. Maybe, Jeanie, you were having a bad dream.

RUTH   Maybe she's just a pest—waking up the whole house! *(Jeanie starts to cry.)*

MOTHER   *(Angry)* That was unkind, Ruth! *(Puts arm around Jeanie)*

JEANIE   Can't we move back to Montclair?

MOTHER   No, Jeanie, we can't move back, but we can do some things to make it easier for you to be here. Tomorrow when we are all wide awake, we are going to talk about it. But right now we must all get some sleep. Good night, Ruthie *(Kisses her.)* Good night, Jeanie. *(Kisses her.)* *(Both say "Good night, Mother.")*

RUTH   You can come into my bed if you want, Jeanie.

JEANIE   O.K. Good night, Ruthie. *(Moves "bed" to Ruthie)*

RUTH   Sleep tight. See you in the morning.

NARRATOR   Now we would like you, the audience, to give us an ending for our play. You may write a composition to describe what happened the morning after Jeanie's nightmare; or you may put your ideas into the form of a third act for our play and our actors will perform it.

Before you compose an ending to the play, let us discuss Jeanie and her problem.

Discussion "Thank you, children. That was a fine presentation.

"We can see that Mother, Bob and Ruth were able to accept the move to a new home. Why wasn't Jean able to?

"Were Bob and Ruth helpful to their sister?

"What do you think Jean's "gorilla"dream meant?

"What were some of Jean's fears?

"What can she do about them?

"Does she need her family's help in working out her fears?

"It is normal to want things to remain the same when we feel comfortable and secure. However, life is made up of new experiences and constant change. Sometimes we must make quick decisions about changes. As we grow up and become more mature we are able to accept the new and strange. When we have the help of others we are able to make a satisfactory adjustment to change."

In addition to writing and acting out the third act, some children may want to draw a picture of a scene from the play, or make a film strip, or TV presentation (using a cardboard box and paper towel rollers.)

A child who has had a similar experience may want to write a play about this for classroom interpretation.

Lesson Plan 5

THE MERRY KINGDOM OF TINSELVANIA—A PLAY WITH MASKS

Aims To help children become more expressive public speakers.

To give a valuable psychological life to the shy, depressed, and aggressive children in the class.

Introduction This lesson has a triple-barreled effect. It is fun, motivational for both slow readers and advanced students, and does wonders for the distressed children. Why is it so effective? Because, with masks, no one is looking directly at you or establishing eye contact, which is all too often frightening for some children. According to Dr. Vicki Arden, the eminent San Diego psychologist, masks are an effective means of therapeutic communication. Her studies show that people who find it difficult to speak before others often find themselves at ease with speaking from behind a mask.

If you'd like to add variety to your language arts program, try this lesson around Halloween time. Masks and costumes are more available and motivation is high. The children will love this lesson!

I have embellished this old fairy tale to accommodate more characters for class participation.

Procedure Post the play title on the board a day before the lesson. Add: this will be a mask play. Determine which children are to be selected for each part. If you wish to involve distressed children, remember to choose opposites for the roles. For instance, you may cast these kinds of children for the following roles:

Prince . . . . popular but quiet, generous boy

Playmate. . . . . shy student

Nobles (Counts and

Countesses) . . . . . . three with low self-esteem

King. . . . . good actor, a withdrawn or aggressive child does well here

Wise Old Sage . . . . hostile student

Peasant mother . . . any girl

Jenny. . . . . ⎰ both roles are good for

Edward. . . . . ⎱ any low self-image children

Narrator . . . . any child who needs to develop a more audible voice. Give him this job because he can work at it independently.

Narrator chores can be split. The same person does not have to narrate throughout.

Have a copy of the play for each child in the class. After they have read the fairy tale play, explain that you would like masks to be used.

"Class, we are going to read this play aloud and we will use masks for our characters. Everyone will have a chance to be in the play because we will have two different casts. We will need a few props: a game for the Prince, a throne for the king, table and chairs, dishes, cups, and coffee pot for the peasant home, and, if you like, a walking stick for the sage to lean on.

"Each of you will bring in a mask, and if you wish, a costume that will best portray your part. The mask forces us to use our voice and our body for expression because the mask is set into one pose and cannot be changed. We must impress our audience through the use of our voices and gestures."

After the group has performed, they remove their masks and take a bow together. Audience applauds. Actors return to seats.

Discussion   "I hope you enjoyed our fairy tale play both as audience and actors. I would like you to comment on the actors and how they portrayed who they were from behind their masks."

Add your own comments and praise to what is given. If someone says "I couldn't hear Ann," you can add "Sometimes I couldn't hear her either. Next time I'm sure she'll be much louder." Try to find some good quality about each performer and assure the audience that the next performance will be super.

Try this lesson again after a month or so. There should be improvement and eagerness to perform for another class.

Some classes make their own masks for this lesson as an art project.

THE PLAY: *"The Merry Kingdom of Tinselvania"*

CAST: Narrator
Young Prince Alexander
Playmate
Tutor, Ivar
Wise Old Sage
King Alexander (the Prince 20 years later)

Nobles (about 3)
Peasant Mother
Peasant Neighbor
Peasant Son, Edward
Peasant Daughter, Jenny

Scene I: Palace Courtyard

NARRATOR   Greetings, boys and girls. Our play will take us to the merry old land of Tinselvania in the days of long, long ago. We hope you will enjoy this story of a king and how he solved the problem of keeping his kingdom merry.

You see, the people of Tinselvania believed that if their king was truly happy, they, too, would be happy. If the king was sad, then they, the people, were unhappy too.

The play opens in the palace courtyard where the little prince, who will someday be king, is playing. (*Prince and playmate are playing marbles or simple game.*)

PLAYMATE   Hey, I won that one!

PRINCE   Yes. Want to play again?

PLAYMATE   I'd like to, but I have stayed longer than ever, Your Highness. My family is expecting me.

PRINCE   (*Angrily*) Never mind your family. You stay here and play with me! It's my turn to win!

PLAYMATE   But that's not fair, Prince Alex. I have to go and I don't think I want to play with you any more.

PRINCE   (*Shouting*) Then get out before I have you thrown out! I am the Prince and I do what *I* want to do!

(Playmate shakes head in disbelief and exits. Prince goes into a tantrum as tutor enters.)

TUTOR   Your Highness, I hope you didn't have another fight with a friend.

PRINCE   *(Still angry)* He's a cheater! He wouldn't let me win! I hate him!

TUTOR   Oh, no! That was the last young Baron that we could find to play with you. The others have refused to come back. You have driven all your friends away. Now what do we do, Prince?

PRINCE   They were a bunch of lugheads.

TUTOR   No they weren't. They gave you every chance to show that you could be a friendly prince.

PRINCE   *(Stomps at tutor)* Ivar! You're not the boss over me! I'm going to tell my father that you are mean and that you push me around. I'm going to get you out of the palace! *(Exits)*

End Scene I

NARRATOR   What kind of man do you think our young Prince Alex will grow up to be? His father and mother were jolly people and they had a merry kingdom. Because they were fair rulers the people were generally happy. When Alex became King, life in the kingdom changed. Let us look in at the palace many years later. Alex is now the king.

Scene II: The Palace, many years later.

KING   *(Stomping back and forth across the stage, still*

angry) Why am I so miserable? Why? Why? I don't have a friend. No one loves me. Loves me? No one even likes me. Every princess and lady-in-waiting makes believe she is engaged so she won't have to see me and talk to me. I feel that they despise my presence. *(Sadly)* Maybe I had better humble myself and call upon the wise old Sage. *(Rings bell and continues to walk back and forth until Sage appears)*

SAGE   *(Excited, bows low)* Your Majesty, to what or to whom do I owe the honor of being called to you? In the ten years of your reign I have never before been asked to share my wisdom with you.

KING   *(Impatient)* I know, I know. My father used to consult with you often. Well, wise old Sage, I am going to see if you can help me now. My people don't like me and I can't figure out why. *(Sarcastically)* Do you think you can do something for me, old man?

SAGE   *(Calmly)* Maybe yes, maybe no.

KING   *(Angry)* What do you mean, "maybe"?! Either it's yes or no!

SAGE   *(Still calm)* I say "maybe" because everything depends upon you. Only you can make a decision to change yourself.

KING   *(Snarls)* I don't need to change. I just want to know how to make the people of my kingdom friendly toward me. Shall I give them each a ticket to the great fair?

SAGE   *(Firmly)* The rule of friendship is: To have a friend you must first be one. It says nothing about presents, your majesty. One cannot buy a friend, one must become a friend.

KING   I don't know how to become a friend, old Sage. What must I do?

SAGE   *(Walks back and forth across stage chanting)* Learn this chant: I must share, be fair, and care. *(King joins Sage and they walk and chant together. For the first time, the King smiles.)*

KING   Listen, old Sage, is this the way it goes? I must share, be fair, and care? *(Both exit, chanting and clapping to the beat.)*

Scene III: The Palace, a month later.

NARRATOR   It looks like His Majesty, Alexander, is not such a bad king! If he sticks to his cranky old ways, then the kingdom will be filled with angry people. But if he changes his ways, there will be great rejoicing! The whole kingdom will be a merry one!

In our next scene the King has summoned his nobles to help him gain the friendship of his people.

COUNT(ESS) BAROON   *(Amazed)* The King has never asked our advice before. What is the meaning of this strange new behavior?

COUNT(ESS) TATOON   *(Skeptical)* I don't trust him past my nose. The nasty old villain must have something up his sleeve!

COUNT(ESS) ZAZOON   *(Greets King, bows low; others bow, too)* Your Majesty!

KING   Good day, Baroon, Tatoon, and Zazoon. I have called this meeting to ask your help. If our kingdom is to become a merry one, I must become a friendly king. I need to witness the good deeds of some of my people who are merry and friendly. My command is that you go out among the people and find a family that can share, be fair, and care about each other. They can live here in the palace and teach me to share, be fair, and care about people. Do you think this is a good idea?

BARROON, TATOON, ZAZOON   Oh, yes, Your Majesty. A wonderful plan!

KING   Then make your way and be back here in one month. Safe journey to all of you! *(Exits)*

TATOON   Humph. . . . The king and his idea are dumb!

BAROON   Humph. . . . All of a sudden I feel glum.

ZAZOON   Humph. . . . All I can say is "Ho-hum." *(The three nobles exit chanting: "Share, be fair, and care," "Share, be fair, and care. . .")*

NARRATOR   The three nobles each took a different section of the kingdom through which to travel. While they are searching for friendly merry people, let us look into a peasant cottage in a small village many miles from the palace.

Scene IV: Peasant cottage.

MOTHER   *(Standing)* Will you have more coffee, neighbor Blacksmith?

NEIGHBOR   *(Seated)* Just a little and then I must go home. It is almost sundown.

MOTHER   *(Pours coffee and sits)* Edward and Jenny are late getting home today. They walked to the village. Jenny heard of a Baroness who is seeking a dressmaker and Edward went with her so that Jenny would not have to go alone.

NEIGHBOR   *(Finishes coffee, rises)* You are blessed with those wonderful children, neighbor Allman. Not every widow has such good fortune. *(Puts on jacket)*

MOTHER   Yes, I am blessed. Soon the day will come when Jenny will leave home for a job in the village, and I must face the day when Edward goes out into the world. Such a fine craftsman cannot work on this little farm forever.

NEIGHBOR   True, true. Well I must be on my way now. Thank you, neighbor Allman, the coffee was delicious.

MOTHER   Good day, neighbor. My regards to your family. *(Neighbor exits. Mother busies herself in kitchen. Enter Jenny and Edward very excited.)*

JENNY   Mother, wait till you hear what happened! *(Edward is removing coat.)* We met Count(ess) Zazoon and he will be here soon to meet you!

MOTHER   Coming here?!? Tell me about it. Are you children in trouble?

EDWARD   No, mother. This is what happened. Jenny and I were walking home when we were stopped by a finely dressed noble person with a servant. Their coach had broken down. They were lost and looking for the village inn. Jenny and I decided to walk with them and show them the inn. The Count(ess) talked with us all the way and then offered us money for our help.

MOTHER   You refused the money, I hope.

JENNY   Of course, mother. Then he offered us both jobs at the palace!

EDWARD   But we refused.

MOTHER   How could you refuse? It seems like a dream.

EDWARD   Mother, we would never leave you here alone.

MOTHER   Nonsense, you must seize the opportunity.

JENNY   Mother, we wouldn't think of it. We had fun just meeting a noble person.

EDWARD   Count(ess) Zazoon will have dinner and then he will hire a new coach and ride out here. I guess he wants to explain to you why we were late and thank us.

JENNY   I am so hungry.

MOTHER   Well, I have a fine lamb stew with dumplings for us. *(All are seated at table, dinner is eaten.)*

EDWARD   *(Very serious)* It doesn't look like Jenny will get the seamstress job. They want a dressmaker who also makes household linens and laces.

JENNY   Whoever takes that job will be almost blind in a few years. I'd rather stay here until something I want comes along.

MOTHER   A person should be happy about his job. *(There's a knock at the door.)*

EDWARD   Are they here already? I'll answer it. Welcome, Count(ess). Please come in. *(Mother and Jenny rise to greet Noble)* This is my mother, Mrs. Allman. Mother, this is Count(ess) Zazoon.

MOTHER   I bid you welcome, your lordship (ladyship). Will you have some dinner with us?

ZAZOON   Thank you, madam. There is no time. I must go back immediately to the palace. My servant was able to get a coach and we will stop for dinner on our journey back.

MOTHER   Then it was kind of you to stop here.

ZAZOON   Madam, I will be brief. For the past month I have journeyed thoughout the southern part of Tinselvania to find a friendly person or family to bring to the king. They had to prove that they could share, be fair, and care. Your children certainly fit that description. I have chosen your children and you to come to the palace and help make the king merry. *(Jenny and Edward are delighted.)*

MOTHER   We are poor peasants without education. I cannot read or write.

ZAZOON   That will not matter to the king. The wise old Sage has convinced him that the highest form of wisdom is understanding. Certainly you are an understanding person madam.

JENNY   Mother, let's go. I can't wait to see the king. He's very handsome, I hear.

EDWARD   Count(ess) Zazoon, my mother is as thrilled as my sister and I are. I'll talk her into it.

ZAZOON   (Smiling) Good! A coach will pick you up in three days. Bring only what you will need to wear for one week. The king must approve of you. And now, I must go. Good night, Madam Allman *(slight bow)*, Edward *(shakes hands)*, Jenny *(slight bow)*.

MOTHER AND JENNY   Safe journey, your lordship. *(After Count[ess] leaves, Mother and Jenny hug each other, exclaiming "the palace, the palace!" (Edward scratches head in disbelief.)*

NARRATOR   Can you imagine the excitement that followed? Now we take you back to the palace for our final scene.

Scene V: (Old Sage enters with the three nobles.)

TATOON   There is music in the air.

BAROON   Yes. *(Turns to Sage)* What magic have you done, Old Sage, to make the sad king a merry king?

SAGE   No magic of mine. The king has made his own magic. He wanted to change and he did. I suggested and he tried out a different way of acting and being.

TATOON   Whatever, whatever, 'tis better than ever. *(Enter king; takes place on throne)*

KING   Good morning to all. I am anxiously awaiting the results of your trips to find a merry person in our kingdom. Baroon, how did you fare?

BAROON   *(Frightened, shaking)* Not well, Your Majesty. In all the north I could not find a merry person.

KING   That is too bad. You seem afraid to tell me this. Don't be afraid. Maybe Tatoon had better luck?

TATOON   *(Frightened, shaking)* Your majesty, I spoke to every noble and peasant in the midland and not one fit the pattern of "share, be fair, and care."

KING   *(Discouraged)* I am sure you tried your best, Tatoon. Perhaps the task was too difficult. After so many years of a cranky kingdom, I guess the disease of crankiness has infected everyone.

SAGE   We have yet to hear from Count(ess) Zazoon. *(Zazoon enters followed by Mrs. Allman, Jenny, and Edward. They bow to king. He nods.)*

ZAZOON   Your Majesty. I present for your consideration the Allman family. They do share, they are fair, and they care!

KING   How is this evident, Zazoon? *(Zazoon tells story of his encounter with Jenny and Edward. King is impressed.)* It's been a long time since I have heard of such kindness done with a pleasing manner. I am pleased. If you come to live at the palace, then I can learn from you and become a merry king. My merriness will multiply and soon Tinselvania will be the merriest kingdom in the world! Will you stay?

MOTHER JENNY EDWARD   *(Bow)* We will be honored. *(All on stage applaud.)*

KING   Then I will give a great feast. Come with me now, Allman family; we will prepare. *(Exit king and family; others shake heads in disbelief.)*

BAROON   The king seems to be merry and gay!

ZAZOON   Let's hope it will last, I pray!

SAGE   Merry forever and a day!

TATOON   I think I'll faint, if I may! *(Feigns weakness)*

END

Lesson Plan 6
"HELLO, MY NAME IS MR. OBSEQUIOUS."

Aims   To practice new vocabulary words.

To make a role-play game of vocabulary learning.

Procedure   Make, or have the children make some "Hello, my name is" cards. Cut out circles four inches in diameter and with a magic marker print "Hello, my name is" around the top. Draw a line across the middle.

Each day the teacher or the children suggest words that could go on the cards. Try to choose important and unusual words. Each child fills in a word on his card and then pins the card on his shoulder. As they meet each other or other children on the playground during the day's activities, they ask each other and are asked to show what their name means. The child wearing the tag acts out the answer. The questioner then gives a definition or uses the word in a sentence. The child with the name tag tells if it's right.

The teacher may want to offer some practice in class first. For example: I have a name card here for Mr. Alternative. Will he please stand up? Show us what your name means. Can you dramatize it? Who can give a synonym? Who can use the word in a sentence? Good, you can pin this name tag on for today.

Discussion   Choose words that portray character traits, feelings (e.g. downcast, elated), sensory perceptions (e.g. fragile, sultry, tender). Never let a child be tagged with a word that does happen to characterize him if it has negative connotations (e.g. hostile, obstinate).

Lesson Plan 7
SPELLING DIALOGUES

Aims   To make a game of an activity that is generally onerous.

To combine spelling with creative writing.

Procedure   Have each child pick a partner. Assign each pair a short list of words. The children are to create their own playlets, using the assigned words. They can write out their script. The assigned words will be spelled out; the rest of the words spoken. Actors get up and read their script to the class. They then call on the audience to identify and re-spell the words. Example:

BOB   I sure do like S-P-O-R-T-S.

JOHN   Me too. My F-A-V-O-R-I-T-E game is baseball.

BOB   Are you on the V-A-R-S-I-T-Y team?

JOHN   Yes, and we won the P-E-N-N-A-N-T last year.

Discussion   The teacher will have made up the word lists in advance, choosing spelling words that have come up in language, reading, and social studies. The words are grouped in categories so that they will suggest possibilities for conversation to the children. Examples:

suspense	facilities	traffic	injection
character	community	emergency	poodle
channel	recreation	accident	medicine
program	neighborhood	witness	veterinarian

The same list may be given to several pairs of children. They will all enjoy seeing the different scripts they come up with.

Lesson Plan 8
CHORAL SPEAKING: GREEN BROOM AND A LAUGHING CHORUS

Aims   To encourage clear and rhythmic speech.

To give children who are too shy to speak alone an opportunity to perform in a group without embarrassment.

To enjoy old chants, ballads, poems.

Procedure   The exact procedure will of course depend on the selection. It is a good idea for the whole class to read the poem through silently first. (Use an overhead transparency or give each child a mimeographed copy.)

To help the children feel the rhythmic flow of the poem, the teacher should conduct a few lines for practice, setting the rhythm slowly and deliberately: and a one, and a two, and a three, let's go—"There was an old man," etc. Impress upon children the need to speak in unison, clearly, enunciating each word carefully.

For *Green Broom*, divide the class into two groups for the dark voices and the light voices. Select one girl to read the woman part. Select a boy for the part of Johnny and one for the old man. They may pantomime appropriate actions as the chorus speaks.

For *Laughing Chorus* there are no individual parts. Just divide the class into six groups and follow the same plan as for *Green Broom*.

Green Broom

ALL

There was an old man lived out in the wood
  Whose trade was the cutting of Broom, green Broom;
He had but one son without thrift, without good,
  Who lay in his bed till 'twas noon, bright noon.

DARK VOICES

The old man awoke one morning and spoke.
  He swore he would fire the room, that room,
If his John would not rise and open his eyes,
  And away to the wood to cut Broom, green Broom.

LIGHT VOICES

So Johnny arose, and slipped on his clothes,
  And away to the wood to cut Broom, green Broom;
He sharpened his knives, and for once he contrived
  To cut a great bundle of Broom, green Broom.

ALL

When Johnny passed by a fine lady's house,
   Passed under a lady's fine room, fine room,
She called to her maid,

WOMAN

Go fetch to my side,
   Go fetch me the boy that sells Broom, green Broom.

ALL

Johnny came into that lady's fine house,
   And stood in that lady's fine room, fine room;

WOMAN

Young Johnny my lad, will you give up your trade,
   And marry a lady in bloom, full bloom?

ALL

John gave his consent and to church they both went,
   And he married the lady in bloom, full bloom.
At market and fair all the folks do declare,
   There's none like the boy that sold Broom, Green
   Broom.

—OLD BALLAD

A Laughing Chorus

I

ALL

Oh, such a commotion under the ground
   When March called, "Ho, there! ho!"
Such spreading of rootlets far and wide,
   Such whispering to and fro.

GROUP 1

And "Are you ready?" the Snowdrop asked;
  "'Tis time to start, you know."

GROUP 2

"Almost, my dear," the Daisy replied;
  "I'll follow as soon as you go."

ALL

Then, "Ha! ha! ha!" a chorus came
  Of laughter soft and low
From the millions of flowers under the ground—
  Yes—millions—beginning to grow.

(Pause)
II

GROUP 3

"I'll promise my blossoms," the Crocus said,
  "When I hear the bluebirds sing."

ALL

And straight thereafter Narcissus cried,

GROUP 4

"My silver and gold I'll bring."

GROUP 5

"And ere they are dulled," another spoke,
  "The Hyacinth bells shall ring."

GROUP 6

And the Marigold murmured, "I'm here,"
  And sweet grew the air of spring.

ALL

Then, "Ha! ha! ha!" a chorus came
  Of laughter soft and low

From the millions of flowers under the ground—
   Yes—millions—beginning to grow.

(Pause)
III

ALL

Oh, the pretty, brave things! through the coldest days,
   Imprisoned in walls of brown,
They never lost heart, though the blast shrieked loud,
   And the sleet and the hail came down.

GROUPS 1, 2, 3:

But patiently each wrought her beautiful dress,
   Or fashioned her beautiful crown;

GROUPS 4, 5, 6:

And now they are coming to brighten the world,
   Still shadowed by winter's frown;

ALL

And well may they cheerily laugh, "Ha! ha!"
   In a chorus soft and low,
The millions of flowers hid under the ground—
   Yes—millions—beginning to grow.

      — ANONYMOUS

Discussion　The poems above, and many others, will be found in Elizabeth Keppies' book *Choral Verse Speaking*, Boston, Mass., Expression Co., 1956.

Lesson Plan 9
PANTOMIME: *THE ELVES AND THE HAT SELLER*

Aims　To spontaneously convert words into actions as a story is being read.

To encourage creative expression.

To impress children with the effectiveness of non verbal communication.

Procedure　Have children bring in hats of all kinds. Put them in a large box that the hat seller will carry.

Cast four elves, a hat seller and three customers. Teacher reads aloud the following story, adapted from an old fairy tale, after designating who will be customer 1, 2, and 3, and elf 1, 2, 3, and 4. As the teacher reads, the cast dramatizes, using only gestures and actions and no words.

Once upon a time in a far away country there lived a little old man whose name was Dandy Dan. People called him Dandy Dan because he always wore such handsome hats.

Now, Dandy Dan was a hat seller by trade. He went from town to town and door to door selling his beautiful hats.

One day, when he was in the town of Grinstead, he sat with his box of hats in the market place. Soon the first customer of the day stopped by and tried on a few hats. He found one that he liked, but when Dandy Dan told him how much it was he thought it was much too expensive. The customer became so angry that he threw the hat down on the ground.

Poor Dan picked up the hat, dusted it off, put it back with the others.

Soon, the second customer of the day, who almost walked past him as she was in such a hurry, came back to look at the beautiful hats.

Her eyes almost popped out and she clapped her hands in glee. She tried on first this hat and then that hat and back to the first one and then to another one. She just couldn't make up her mind.

Would she buy or not, Dan wondered. She lifted the prettiest one from the display and tried it on admiringly. Suddenly she pointed to something in the other direction. Dan looked and looked but could see nothing. When he turned back, the customer and the hat were gone.

Dan was very sad. He decided to put all his hats in the box and go to another stand. Before he reached what he thought might be a better place, a third customer sauntered up to the box and demanded to be shown everything in the box. Dan took out hat after hat, but nothing would please the customer.

After the customer left, Dan emptied his pockets and found he had only two coins. He put them away, picked up his hats and decided to go into the forest where he could sleep for the night.

Dan walked and walked. At last he saw a comfortable spot where a big pine tree would keep him safe for the night. He set down his box of hats, yawned, then spread out his coat, curled up on it and fell fast asleep.

He wasn't asleep too long when some little elves tiptoed around to look at the sleeping figure. They shook their heads in disbelief. Very seldom did they ever see a human being.

They tiptoed over to the box of hats and one by one they took out the hats. They didn't know quite what to do with them. One elf thought it must belong on a foot, while another tried a hat on his elbow. A third elf thought you must have to punch a hole in it but the fourth, who was the wisest elf, tried it on his head. It seemed to fit and the other elves looked at him and roared with laughter.

Then they all wanted to try the different hats on. They had never seen anything so funny in all their lives. To add to their glee they each donned a hat, took hands and skipped around in a circle.

They almost forgot about Dan who had begun to stir in his sleep. But the wise elf looked over at Dan and realized that he was waking up. Dan yawned and stretched and couldn't believe his eyes when he saw four elves staring at him and wearing his hats. This was too much for Dan to take!

He got up and demanded that his hats be given back. But the elves didn't understand the human's language. Dan grabbed a hat from one of the elves and put it back in the box. The other elves looked at each other and began to cry. They wanted the hats.

This amused Dan and he began to feel kindly toward the little elves. He tried to explain to them that the hats had to be exchanged for gold.

The elves looked at each other. Finally the wise elf stepped forward. He reached into his pocket and brought out a bag of beautiful gold nuggets. It was more gold than Dan had ever seen. He picked out what he thought to be a fair trade but the wise elf insisted he take all.

Dan bowed very low and joined hands with the elves. They danced around and around together. Soon Dan said goodbye. The elves were happy with their hats and Dan really felt like "Dandy Dan" as he went off.

Discussion   Teacher should read slowly and pause long enough for action to take place. The class audience will giggle now and then. Teacher should be cautious to wait until the sounds of laughter die down before continuing the narration.

For later performances of this, as well as of other pantomime plays, the teacher may choose a student to be the narrator.

Some of the older classes have enjoyed doing pantomime shows so much that they were inspired to write their own scripts and put on performances for the younger classes.

Lesson Plan 10
SO, YOU'D LIKE TO PRODUCE A PLAY.

Aims   To apply the skills children (and teacher) have developed in role-playing to the more formal production of a play.

To perform before a live audience.

To interpret and project to others the characters in a story.

To project speech and actions clearly and dramatically.

To remember and reproduce dialogue and plot.

Procedure 1. Selection of Play—Select a play that will use most of the class. Some will be actors and some stage crew. A play with only one or two scene changes will simplify things.

Have enough scripts for the cast plus a few extras. There will always be lost scripts.

The completed play should be timed for a maximum of 20-35 minutes. A longer play would be too ambitious for a first try.

Discuss the play with the class. They have to like it and want to take part in it.

Consider the resources needed. How will you manage the scenery, lighting, and costumes?

2. Casting—Director, appointed by teacher or chosen by children, can decide upon the cast. In some cases, class can vote for leads. This removes some of the burden of selection from the teacher.

3. Rehearsal Schedule—Planning for those not in a scene is just as important as planning to rehearse the actors. In the beginning, the entire class is interested in the action onstage, but after repeated performances they become a little weary. Give them some work to do while rehearsal is in progress. It may be related to the play—*e.g.* making theater bills, sewing costumes, and making backdrops. Or it may be unrelated.

4. Rehearse Act I Only. This is called "blocking." Have one act well under way before starting the next. Each child should have a play copy so that he doesn't have to borrow copies from others. The first few run-throughs are with benefit of script. No attention is paid to movement or stage placement. Actors will need someone at home to help them memorize lines. A good

technique is for the prompter to read the line just ahead of the line the rehearsing actor is to speak. Gradually, as memorization takes place, the stage movement is introduced.

How long rehearsing Act I will take depends upon the rate at which the children memorize. An average group can do this in a week to ten days.

Fifteen minutes of rehearsal per day is better than one hour twice a week. Monday is usually difficult. The weekend has provided time for forgetting.

Makeshift scenery is used for early rehearsals. Stage crew sets up before rehearsal begins. Teacher chooses a member of crew to be the reader. Reader cues in an actor who forgets a line by reading a small portion of the forgotten line.

5. Acts II, III—Same procedure as Act I.

6. First Run-through of Entire Play—Stage crew sets up scenery. Reader sits near cast ready to cue. Actors take their places. Rest of cast waits for entrance cues, with one of the stage crew maintaining order and silence.

No matter how disorganized things may seem, the first run-through should be just that—a run-through with no interruptions by the director and no actor stopping to ask a question. It's the play straight through from beginning to end. The director (and teacher) may make notes about the weak spots that need help.

7. Problem Spots—Following the first run-through, iron out rough spots by discussion with the entire class. How can we improve Melanie's part? Were you able to hear John in the back of the room? What did you like about the play? Any constructive suggestions?

If any child is giving an inappropriate performance, speak to him privately and offer to help.

8. Second Run-through—Do not move a play from classroom to auditorium stage without a rehearsal first. The stage space is completely different and often the new atmosphere causes insecure performances. Also lost are voice depth and movement. What looks good in a smaller, more intimate classroom can give a totally different picture on a stage.

Stage crew take their places.

Announcer takes his place. Play begins and runs right through, presumably more smoothly this time.

Discussion follows.

Costumes are discussed and assignments made. Date is set for Costume Dress Rehearsal.

9. Costume Dress Rehearsal—Never, never give a performance without a dress rehearsal at least two days before the performance. Wearing a costume changes the stage movement and placement for the actors. For example, a child cast as a soldier may wear a helmet that can fall off during the performance, or may have a sword that doesn't come out at the proper time. Costume problems have turned many a serious play into a farce and caused disappointment for the actors. Leave enough time between the dress rehearsal and the final performance to straighten out costume problems. A performance slated for the latter part of the week is likely to be more successful.

10. Invitation Performance—Children may make invitations for parents and friends who might attend the play. (Children under four can ruin the performance with their innocent noises. Avoid if possible.)

Schedule the play for late morning or late afternoon. Doing a show generates excitement and it is virtually impossible to settle down to ordinary class work when the children are still high with excitement from the play.

At the end of the play, each and every child who participated in the overall effort should be announced by name and should take a bow. This is a very important aspect of the value of giving a play. Taking bows can be rehearsed the day before the performance.

After the play is over, a question and answer session between parents and cast is fun. This reinforces the importance of being a part of the play.

Discussion   There are no stars. Each participant is a vital cell of the living body of a play.

The teacher sets the ground rules for discipline before starting rehearsals. Infraction of ground rules is cause for dismissal from cast. (No "one more chances").

1. Be prepared. Any person coming to rehearsal without his script two times will be replaced.

2. Respect the right of others to stumble through lines in the beginning rehearsals.

3. Any person lax in job of memorizing who doesn't seek help will be replaced.

4. No actor should ever break character. No one onstage ever waves to someone in the audience or talks to another when he is not delivering a line. Impress upon children that any side action distracts the au-

dience and ruins the performance of the actors who are striving for the audience's attention.

Putting on a play can be very rewarding and enjoyable. But it is also hard work and requires a great deal of cooperation and self-discipline. Children are often nervous and teacher needs to reassure them enough so that they are relaxed, but not so much that they are too casual and careless.

Answer whatever questions children ask, even if they seem absurd. It is not unusual for questions like "Do the boys have to wear lipstick?" to try the teacher's patience. Treat every serious question seriously.

Doing a play is an involving, encompassing and tension producing activity. Expect a few flare-ups, temper tantrums and misunderstandings.

Set a relaxed mood and the children will capture it. The teacher who says to a child, "Now don't be nervous" is really instilling a doubt in this child's mind. He muses, "There must be something I ought to be nervous about." Such comments as "How do you feel? Are you scared?" do not belong.

Don't expect perfection. Keep calm, sustain your enthusiasm and enjoy the children's efforts.

One final practical hint—see that children go to the bathroom before getting into costume for performance.

SOCIAL STUDIES

A child's sense of time and distance evolves slowly as he matures and accumulates experiences. The vocabulary and concepts of geography and history are often abstract and remote from the child's reality. Role-play can make an important contribution to the child's understanding by converting past into present, dead characters into living personalities, an irrelevant array of facts into meaningful issues and conflicts. Presented here are but a few suggestions; social studies teachers will have many ideas for using these techniques.

Children enjoy improvising short scenes from history after studying and discussing a unit. The teacher may bring to life any reenactment from the pages of history—the building of a pyramid, the life of an ancient Spartan, the experiences of a Crusader, an explorer, a colonizer of America, Columbus petitioning aid from Queen Isabella, etc.

After the class has worked on a unit, a series of role-play situations may be improvised dealing with various aspects studied. This will give the teacher a better idea of what and how much and how well the children have absorbed information than any number of tests or quizzes.

Lesson Plan 1
WE LAND ON PLYMOUTH ROCK.

Aims   To recreate an historical experience.

To imagine how people felt in a new and perilous situation.

Introduction   "Can you imagine how the Pilgrims felt when they arrived on our shores? Try to picture in your mind what it was like. Were they feeling scared? Happy? Perhaps lonely? Sad? What did they talk about? Let's make believe we are those Pilgrims. Who would like to be on that boat?"

Procedure Children will have ideas and will improvise dialogue to recreate the scene. Perhaps they would like some time to prepare hats, and other props.

Discussion The teacher should guide children by posing "feeling" questions, which are as important and less threatening than "fact" questions. Several groups may portray the same scene.In the discussion following the action, the facts may be brought out by comparing performances, but the primary rule for improvisation should be: Feelings first, facts follow!

As a follow-up role-play situation, the children might enjoy using the Rip Van Winkle idea. A TV reporter has come upon Priscilla, who, miraculously, has just awakened after having been asleep since 1612. The reporter and Priscilla stage a spontaneous interview for a 1975 audience.

Lesson Plan 2
LET'S TAKE A TOUR.

Aims To stimulate curiosity about the wide, wide world.

To share information and/or experience acquired about far away places and foreign customs.

To ask and answer pertinent questions about places of interest.

Procedure   One of the most successful forms of dramatizing subject matter is by role-playing a tour guide taking a group of travellers through an important city or place of interest. If the class has had a visitor from a distant place, or has studied about a place of interest, or if a pupil has taken a trip with his family, a simulated role-play can be initiated.

An interesting scene was planned by a ten-year-old girl who had visited Disneyland. She chose a tour group of six students and took them on an imaginary visit to the attractions she had enjoyed most. During the trip they asked questions which she answered to the best of her ability. Following the ten-minute tour, the teacher and class offered additional experiences and information.

A sixth-grade class studying Switzerland chose to act out the following scene: a Swiss shepherd turned over his mountain chalet to a group of skiers for the winter season.

The children chose a director who selected the cast. They worked together combining their ideas, which the director noted on index cards. Two "sheep" were added to the cast. Two rehearsals were held during free time, and costumes and props were agreed upon. Two days later the five-minute play was performed to a captive but highly receptive audience. The actors had worked completely independently. Their object was to get across to the audience the concept of a multi-purpose dwellings in Switzerland. The lesson became an enjoyable and unforgettable experience, with the point well made.

Third-graders are enthusiastic actors when given the opportunity to play the roles of community authority figures. "I am Bill Jones, a policemen. Let me take you on a tour of my beat." "I am Sue Davis, a nurse at Valley Hospital. Let me show you around.""I am Mark Cassin, a fireman. Would you like to see our firehouse?"

Discussion   Give the children time to research their roles, to bring in costumes if they wish, and prepare their speeches. It is hard to put yourself in someone else's shoes, especially if you're trying to show off how important and knowledgeable you are.

Sometimes, you needn't go very far afield for a subject for a tour role-play activity. If the class is composed of different ethnic or religious groups, you can draw on the children's own knowledge and experience of their own cultural and religious customs. Children from different backgrounds can take the class on a (real or role-played) tour of their home or neighborhood explaining customs, traditions, symbols familiar to them but new or strange to others.

Lesson Plan 3
WAS IT A GOOD SHOW? WAS IT A BAD SHOW?

Television is one of the most powerful and pervasive sources of "education" today. Educators cannot be present to oversee the television programs their students are exposed to. Instead of bemoaning the poor quality of television programing, the teacher can make children aware and critical of what is being taught to them on television.

Aims   To evaluate the quality of TV shows.

To differentiate between fact and propaganda in television shows.

To become aware of both overt and hidden propaganda disseminated on TV.

Procedure   Divide the class into groups of three or four simply by having the youngsters count off. One person in each group takes on the job of chairman. Give each group time and a place to meet together, and instruct them to select a television program or commercial to watch at home that evening. The chairman supervises the discussion and records the decision.

The following day, the groups meet again in different parts of the room. They discuss the scene from the show they chose to watch, and prepare to recreate it for the class. Allow groups about 15 minutes for planning, casting, and decisions, although the role-play action time will only be about three minutes. Each chairman notifies the teacher when his group is ready, but all stop at the end of 15 minutes, whether or not they have finished.

The teacher then announces: "Let's return to our seats for group presentation of television shows or commercials. When the action is over we will discuss what made this a good show or a poor show. Which group would like to be first?"

Discussion   "Thank you, Group. How many of you watch this program regularly?

"How many of you like the program?

"How many do not like the program?

"What things in this program could actually happen?

"Are there any things in the show that couldn't possibly happen or are far-fetched?

"If you were a television critic, would you recommend this show to other children?

"What might you tell them to think about as they watch television?"

As a follow-up, assign children to watch a specific program such as "All In The Family" or "Six Million Dollar Man." Ask a few children to be on a panel and chair them in a critical discussion of issues related to the program, e.g. how Archie views people of other races, nationalities, and religions, the probability of the theme of science fiction shows.

Upper grades might watch newscasts with a critical ear towards bias in newscasting. The same can be done to detect bias in sportscasting.

Younger children do well acting out commercials. Teacher may question them about the assertions in television advertising.

Lesson Plan 4

"THIS IS STATION WAAB—THE STATION WITH THE NEWS."

Aims   To present a television newscast.

To imagine a future, ten years from now.

To stimulate creative writing through role-playing.

To promote the skill of reading with expression to an audience.

Procedure   Select children to be the news team. Cast an anchor man, a weatherman, a sportscaster, a theater critic, a foreign correspondent, and a people-in-the-news reporter. They are to write their news reports as if it were ten years in the future. They are to use the names of their classmates as often as possible. The news team can work in groups or individually.

For the final presentation, each child should be limited to two minutes. The anchor man will announce the program and call on each newscaster in turn to read his report to the listening audience. Anchor man will signal when the two minutes are almost up.

Discussion   This is a project that the children enjoy managing independently, doing whatever research and planning they need to do. The end product will be a surprise to class and teacher and should be applauded vigorously.

Lesson Plan 5
LADIES AND GENTLEMEN, WELCOME TO OUR UNICEF MEETING.

Aims   To learn about an international political organization's functioning.

To role-play the representatives of other countries.

To gain awareness of the problems and programs affecting children in many lands.

To argue reasonably and effectively for or against a point of view.

Procedure   Class researches the conditions and problems of children living in other countries. Problem areas might be educational, cultural, or social. In addition to whatever books, periodicals, films, and filmstrips the school and/or public library might provide, the class might gather materials by writing to the United Nations, New York City, New York.

Direct interviewing of children who may have come from another country gives more personal information and may give a child who needs it the opportunity to shine as the authority.

When the information is in, select children to play the representatives of the various countries they researched. More than one representative for a place is fine. A chairman is needed to conduct the session and call on each representative.

If they wish, children can wear native clothes—sari, dashiki, turban, etc.

Simulate the UN Assembly Room by setting up rows of chairs in a semi-circle for observers, and a table on stage where representatives sit. Chairman is seated at table in middle chair.

The teacher sets the scene, lending it importance and dignity: "Class, the day has finally arrived for our meeting of the UN Children's Fund representatives. Let's imagine that each of us has arrived from a different corner of the earth and we are now in glorious New

York City. We are getting out of a taxi. We see the beautiful colored flags of many countries waving in the breeze, and the tall concrete buildings behind them. As we walk up the steps, we see many people hurrying in and out of the buildings. Some are tourists, some are workers, some are from countries far away. As we enter, a friendly guide meets us and conducts us to the Assembly Room for our UNICEF meeting. We take our places and make ourselves comfortable. The representatives take their places around the table. The chairman calls the meeting to order and then calls upon the representatives of each country, one by one, to talk briefly about problems of children in their countries. When the presentation is finished, the chairman asks for comments and suggestions from representatives and observers.

Discussion   The teacher becomes one of the observers. The chairman is responsible for the timing and smooth running of the meeting. What the children have learned will soon become apparent. Later on, interesting ways of making further use of this information may occur to the children (e.g. publishing the minutes of the meeting, polling the school on their reactions to the proposals of the representatives.)

Lesson Plan 6
HOW CAN I TELL YOU? LET ME COUNT THE WAYS.

Aims   To explore the various means of communication.

To discover the advantages and limitations of the various communications media.

To impress children with the importance of communicating with others.

Procedure   "Class, you know we are lucky to live in an age in which there are many means of communication available to us. If you wanted to get a message to someone, what are the different ways you could do it?

"Today we are going to try something together that I think you will find interesting. I will supply you with a message and your task will be to use all the different media to get this message across.

"Here is the message: 'Many people would like our school to have a swimming pool. There will be a meeting of all those who would like to discuss this in the school auditorium on Wednesday afternoon at two o'clock.' "

The teacher can list the different media of communication on the blackboard (or on paper) and the children can sign up for the one they would like to work with. Each group will be given a place and time to get together to plan their presentation.

The presentation can be scheduled for later that day, or the next day, to give the groups time to prepare their work. The final presentations should be limited to three minutes each.

The media to choose from include:

WRITTEN	ORAL
1. letter	1.. telephone
2. book	2. radio
3. magazine	3. face-to-face, two people
4. newspaper	4. face-to-face, a group
5. poster	5. play

VISUAL	MIXED
1. picture(s)	1. TV
2. silent movie	2. sound movie
3. pantomime	3. captioned filmstrip
4. dance	

Discussion   "Which presentations did you find the most interesting? Informative? Easiest to understand? Difficult to understand?

"Which were easy to prepare? Hard to prepare?

"Why is it important to communicate with others? Which media seem to be most likely to give accurate information? Which media stress feelings?

"Would you like to try this exercise again with a different message and with an audience from another class?"

Lesson Plan 7
"MOM, I WANT TO LEAVE HOME."

Aims   To relate an historical event remote in time and space to the real lives of the children.

To suggest an analogy between the child-mother revolt and the colonies' revolt against mother England.

To concretize the idea of the American Revolution.

Procedure   Announce the theme and ask for volunteers to play a role-playing scene for the following day.

Cast two mother-child pairs.

Have the first pair role-play the scene, and follow with the usual discussion.

Before the second group plays the scene, suggest the following: "Boys and girls, we have just seen and discussed what happens when a child revolts against a parent. The parent is bigger and stronger and certainly more powerful. The child is smaller, weaker and has much less power.

"What kinds of power do parents have?

"Do children have any power?

"Now let's compare this problem of a child revolting against Mother with the revolt of the colonies, who were the children against their mother country England. Do you think they are parallel?

"We will go ahead now with the role-play that Mary and Bob have prepared. As you watch them, keep in mind the revolt of the colonies. Later we will discuss similarities between these two situations."

Discussion   Thanks to Libby Ginsburg, a teacher at Chatsworth High School, California, this lesson plan has become a favorite of history teachers who want to show some of the issues involved in the colonies breaking away from mother England.

Lesson Plan 8
BELL OF THE HOUR

Aims   To challenge children to try to use the lessons they learned from studying about famous people in their own lives.

To create an atmosphere of fun while building new values.

To create an immediacy about the determination to change.

Introduction   "We have met many interesting real and imaginary characters as we have read books and studied history. Each one of us probably has a favorite person that we respect and admire. Perhaps we ourselves would like to be more like this person in some way.

"What adjectives would you use to describe Abraham Lincoln? Mary Poppins? Booker T. Washington?"

Procedure   "Today we are going to try a very interesting exercise. This little bell is going to help us.

"Most of the roles that we play in our life are

assigned to us by other people. But there are some roles that we choose ourselves. For instance, if I decide to be a generous person, I will practice being generous. If I decide having a sense of humor is important, I will practice seeing the lighter side of things.

"No one can make me be what I aim to be but myself. Think about yourself. Are there any qualities that you would like to develop or to change? Are you an impatient person? Would you like to try striving to be more patient? Do you tend to give up too quickly? Would you like to take on the role of a determined person?

"Think about one quality or role you would like to have. How do we change our roles? We will start by giving our concentrated attention to our new role. This little bell will help us. I am going to give it to Charles and every hour on the hour Charles will ring the bell. No matter what we are doing, we will stop for thirty seconds. We will speak in silence to ourselves, reminding ourselves that today we are going to be the active, or patient, or amusing person we want to become. When Charles rings the bell again, we can go back to whatever we were doing.

"We will work on one quality only and do it for several days. You may write down your intention but you do not have to share it unless you want to. At the end of our second day, maybe some of you would like to tell the class whether you experienced any success in this venture. You do not have to tell what the quality is that you are trying to change unless you want to. Just report on your progress."

Discussion   Give the bell to a child who is responsible enough to keep it out of sight and yet will remember to ring it every hour. No comments are to be made during the exercise. Children who want to continue to practice after school should be encouraged.

At the end of the second day, take about 15 minutes for sharing. Some children will report that even though they wanted to practice patience, when an angry situation with a younger sibling occurred they forgot about their wish to improve. Teacher should support them by reminding them that improvement does not happen overnight. It takes constant trial and error for successful role change.

Teacher can borrow Benjamin Franklin's idea of keeping a record of successes and failures. Children can make a calendar or diary for the month. They can mark a successful day with an S and a failure day with an F. If at the end of a week the child sees he has more successes than failures, he is motivated to continue. *All* children should receive a commendation for trying. This exercise is intensely personal and depends upon self-motivation. Praise and encouragement from the teacher can be helpful.

Lesson Plan 9
"AS IF" CHARACTERIZATION

Aims   To act as if characters from history or current events were here.

To help students feel the living presence of the character.

To build values through discussing the motivation of these characters.

Procedure Elicit from children the names of famous characters they have studied. Ask for volunteers to act out some experience of a famous character. The individual or group can choose any character they admire. They can do further research about the person. Then they plan a short presentation in which they act "as if" they were that person. Example: a child who chose Amelia Earhart portrayed her getting ready for her famous flight and trying to convince people that she was capable.

Discussion questions follow the action. e.g. Where did this scene take place? How did the person feel? Why did he do what he did? What kind of person was he? How has he influenced your life?

After a few of these dramatic characterizations have been presented, a different format can be introduced. Using the names of the characters already portrayed and adding others to the list (e.g. John Kennedy, Muhammad Ali, Eleanor Roosevelt, Joe Namath, Roman Gabriel, Billie Jean King) tell the class that you are going to describe a situation and they are to choose characters from the list and act out what the characters would do in the situation described.

For example: You are in Paris, scheduled to make a public appearance that evening. You get a cablegram that your child is very ill.

You are on a plane that is hijacked. The guerillas are holding you hostage and want your government to pay them a large sum for your release.

You are offered a large sum of money (or an important position) if you agree to endorse something you do not really believe in.

The children may work alone or in groups. Give

them time to prepare their presentations. Different characters can enact the same problem. Or different children can portray the same character in different situations.

Discussion   One teacher reported that using this characterization lesson with Amelia Earhart evoked a most interesting discussion. Amelia Earhart became the subject for an argument about the women's liberation movement.

At the beginning, use volunteers only. Resistant students will begin to cooperate after seeing the action and results of earlier presentations. A resistant learner is reluctant to try new learning experiences.

Some teachers with good classroom discipline reported that there were many wisecracks in the beginning. Here is how Robert Acosta, teacher at Chatsworth High School, California, handled that problem: "I had to deal with those few students who chose to make wise remarks. I was able to divert them by simply ignoring them and by praising those students who made appropriate and constructive contributions about the character. Following this, the interested students shushed the noisy ones."

The success of this lesson plan depends upon adequate research of the characters.

Index

Abstract thinking, 154, 158, 160, 161-163, 201-202, 207-208
acceptance, *see* approval; tolerance
accuracy
in communication, 212; in math, 145-147
Acosta, Robert, 218
adult-child interpersonal relationships, 86-88, 103-104. *See also* authority
affection, expression of, 139-140.
aggression, 14, 23, 35, 56, 82, 95 173-185. *See also* hostility
Alcoholics Anonymous, 117
alcoholism, 116-118
Ali, Mohammad, 217
"All in the Family," 207
Allport, Gordon, 127
American Revolution, 213-214
analogies, use of, 213-214
anchor man, role-playing, 207-208
anger, 106, 129, 130-132
role-playing, 30, 31, 32, 55-57, 75-77, 99, 105-106, 120-121, 128-129, 168-169, 176-177
annoyance, role-playing, 118-120
anxiety
relieving, 35, 54, 201; role-playing, 93-94
apathy, 16, 72
applause
as encouragement, 95, 208; to end dramatization, 39, 41, 42, 46
appreciation
expressing, 129; importance of, 131-132; role-playing, 88-90, 110-111
approval, 28, 32, 130-132
how to indicate, 29, 35; need for, 126. *See also* praise
Arden, Dr. Vicki, 173
argument, effective technique of, 208-210

art project, 141, 146, 172, 175, 196-201
scenery building, 141, 196-201
athletes, famous, 217
authority
as threat, 100, 106-108; children acting as, 209; dealing with, 103-104, 106-108; role of, 57, 61, 62; role-playing, 103-104, 106-108, 204-205, 213-214
avoidance, role-playing, 78-79, 104
awareness, developing, *see* psychological skills

Bach, George R., 77
banking, *see* business procedure; math skills
behavior modification, 88. *See also* behavioral change
behavioral change, 15, 88, 127-128, 214-216
attempting, 214-216; motivating, 100, 128-130; role-playing, 173-185
behavioral determinants, 127-128. *See also* behavioral change
bias, in newscasts, 207
bigotry, *see* prejudice
blueprints, reading, 148-149
boasting, *see* bragging
book
as method of communication, 212; as research material, 209. *See also* media; research material
borrowing, role-playing, 118-120
bragging, 125-128
bribery, role-playing, 217-218
Bunker, Archie, 207
business procedures, 141, 147-148, 148-149, 149-150, 151-152. *See also* math skills

Calculating, 148-149, 154-156